D0889773

# LUCKY ME

LUCKYMELUCKYMELUCKYM
MELUCKYMELUCKYMELUC
MEUCKYMELUCKYMELUCK
YMELUCKYMELUCKYMELU
UCKYMELUCKYMELUCKYM
CKYMELUCKYMELUCKYME
MELUCKYMELUCKYMELUC
UCKYMELUCKYMELUCKYM
MELUCKYMELUCKYMELU
LUCKYMELUCKYMELUCKY

# LUCKY ME

A MEMOIR OF CHANGING THE ODDS

## RICH PAUL

### WITH JESSE WASHINGTON

ROC
-
LIT
101

NEW YORK

*Lucky Me* is a work of nonfiction. Some names and identifying details have been changed.

Copyright © 2023 by RPXXIII Media, LLC
Foreword by LeBron James copyright © 2023 by LeBron James

All rights reserved.

Published in the United States by Roc Lit 101, a joint venture between Roc Nation LLC and One World, an imprint of Random House, a division of Penguin Random House LLC, New York.

ONE WORLD is a registered trademark of Penguin Random House LLC.
ROC LIT 101 is a trademark of Roc Nation LLC.

LIBRARY OF CONGRESS CATALOGING-IN-PUBLICATION DATA
Names: Paul, Rich, author.
Title: Lucky me: a memoir / Rich Paul.
Description: New York: Roc Lit 101, [2023]
Identifiers: LCCN 2023008623 (print) | LCCN 2023008624 (ebook) |
ISBN 9780593448472 (hardcover) | ISBN 9780593448489 (ebook)
Subjects: LCSH: Paul, Rich, 1981- | Paul, Rich, 1981—Childhood and youth. |
Sports agents—United States—Biography. | African American boys—Ohio—Cleveland—Biography. |
Glenville (Cleveland, Ohio)—Biography.
Classification: LCC GV734.72.P38 A3 2023 (print) | LCC GV734.72.P38 (ebook) |
DDC 796.06/94092 [B]—dc23/eng/20230808
LC record available at https://lccn.loc.gov/2023008623
LC ebook record available at https://lccn.loc.gov/2023008624

Printed in the United States of America on acid-free paper

RocLit101.com
oneworldlit.com

2 4 6 8 9 7 5 3 1

*Roc Lit 101 logo designed by Greg Mollica*
*Book design by Debbie Glasserman*

In a community where people live in despair and denial, the man who defies the rules and is able to make a living becomes a hero.

—CARL STOKES, THE FIRST BLACK MAYOR OF CLEVELAND, OHIO

# FOREWORD

LEBRON JAMES

There's a story behind the urban legend of how Rich Paul and I became brothers.

The legend is that I saw a little guy I had never met before wearing a rare football jersey in the airport, and I wanted to know where he got it. But the jersey didn't really matter. The minute I met Rich, I knew he was different. He understood me from the jump.

A young Black man can be a lot of things with no judgment from his community—athlete, student, hustler, rapper, father—but what he cannot be is vulnerable. When I met Rich, he saw me as just a kid from Akron, Ohio. He knew that even though the LeBron James thing was starting, I had the same fears and dreams as every other young person who grew up the way we did. It didn't take long for me to realize that Rich is great at paying attention: to people, to the different environments that we move in, to why we feel how we feel. Rich sees things deeply. When Rich looked at me, I didn't have to hide anything. The world was coming at me so fast when I was a teenager, and not just basketball. My first son, Bronny, was on the way. I had no dad and no siblings. My mom was struggling. Rich helped me find my strength in that chaos, a chaos that he knew all too well. Rich never asked me for anything. He didn't care whether I was a future pro or the kid across the street. He just knew I needed his help, and he gave me what I needed most—the space to be vulnerable.

That's why Klutch Sports Group is the best agency in the game. Rich's superpower is understanding what people truly need.

After I was drafted in 2003, Rich spent several years working directly with me and learning about the NBA. Then he spent more years working at an agency and a sportswear brand, learning what works for athletes, and why. When Rich started Klutch in 2012, he was better prepared than anyone to take that step, but so many people still slandered his qualifications. It's straight-up disrespectful when they say, "Rich Paul is only successful because he's doing this with LeBron." That's like saying I don't demand the same excellence from my partners that I demand of myself, or that Rich's other clients don't think for themselves. I don't believe in giving my friends free passes—nobody I work with is "given" anything. Compared with the lawyer types who controlled the representation game before him, Rich had to work ten times harder to succeed, because of what he looks like and what he comes from. The only thing Rich received from me is an opportunity.

Rich and I started out as two young Black men from Northeast Ohio who loved music, fashion, and sports; and whose childhoods had been stalked by crack, guns, darkness, and trauma. We lived in neighborhoods where it felt like the government was working to lock up any Black person it could. We both had single mothers who had to fight a broken system way bigger than themselves. Rich and I didn't become brothers because of a throwback jersey—we bonded through unwavering faith in our moms.

Mothers brought us together, but Rich's relationship with his father is the heart of his story. That story has a lot of loss and struggle, but Rich's dad was also a source of wisdom that Rich has passed on to me and other clients over the years, and now he's sharing it with readers of this book. This is the best kind of wisdom, because it was earned the hard way. Rich always knew he was special, but he didn't know just how much he would be able to accomplish. It's amazing to see my brother in full stride, and for everyone else to see what I always saw in him. So when you flip these pages and witness the kind of pain that we felt growing up, don't flinch. Hard truths make us stronger.

# CONTENTS

Someone like me was never supposed to be in my position.
        I spent the early years of my life sleeping on floors and couches as my mother suffered in the grip of a drug addiction. Running the streets with my generation of lost boys, we chased substitutes for love and slammed into closed doors we could not see. But I was raised by some Gs. The common meaning of that term is *gangster*, but I'm also referring to good men—they were sometimes one and the same. The education I got from everyone and everything around me was a gift that came with a curse—it gave me special powers and left me with unfadable scars. So when that door did crack open for me, no professor or office job could have better prepared me for my next life, the one that's not supposed to happen for a guy who's barely

five-foot-eight and grew up with a pair of dice in one hand and a pistol in the other.

. . .

My next life truly began one summer day in 2014 at the Arrogant Butcher, a restaurant in downtown Phoenix. Eric Bledsoe and I were sharing a lunch of turkey sloppy joe sandwiches and fries when the phone on the table lit up. I looked over at Bled and answered the call. The Phoenix Suns had offered him seven million dollars per year over four years—twenty-eight million dollars total—to play the game of basketball.

This was life-changing money for Bled—and for me. Where I grew up, on the East Side of Cleveland, or where Bled grew up in Birmingham, Alabama, the only way to make even a small fraction of that kind of money was to risk your life. But we were in a different world now. Bled was about to hit his first free-agent jackpot, and I was negotiating my first contract as an official agent for my company, Klutch Sports Group.

I hung up the phone and relayed the offer to Bled. He was twenty-four years old, had just enjoyed a great season for Phoenix and established himself as a cornerstone of the franchise. The smile on his face broadcast happiness and relief. He was ready to sign on the dotted line and get to work.

But I wasn't smiling.

"We're not taking this deal," I said.

Bled is a quiet guy, but I could sense the disappointment beneath his blank expression.

"Here's why," I said. "I don't want you stepping on that court night in and night out, playing against guys who you're better than, guys you're outperforming, but you make less than they do. You deserve way more than twenty-eight million. I don't know exactly how much more, but I'm going to get you what you're worth."

I searched Bled's face for the trust that was so rare in my childhood—and found it. He agreed to turn down the contract offer.

Over the next several months, as we engaged in a standoff with the Suns, most of the NBA world expected us to fail. I heard all the comments: *Rich doesn't know what he's doing. He's crazy to turn down that much money. He's not a real agent. He's just LeBron's friend. Rich is gambling with Bledsoe's future.*

What none of these critics knew is that long before I entered the world of the NBA, I had learned that life is full of gambles. Smart gamblers know how to manage the risks, move with intention and integrity, control what they can control—and in the end, they have the heart to let the dice fall where they may. I'd been gambling my whole life, not for as much money, but for higher stakes. Growing up like I did, gambling was weighing the odds of getting shot if you walked down a hostile block. Gambling was being thirteen years old, taking thousands of dollars from grown men in a craps game, then riding home on my bike. Gambling was giving my mom forty dollars and hoping she didn't use it to get high.

. . .

Like a million other Black kids of my generation, I grew up in what outsiders called a ghetto but we experienced as a war. Those of us who survived that war came out traumatized, but also with a special understanding of the world. Our G.I. Bill was for a college without walls whose curriculum was the lessons we learned on the block, from the mothers we lost and the fathers we found, and from each other. One of the most important things I learned was a set of rules. These rules weren't written down in any books, but they were as real and unforgiving as the concrete under my feet. If you broke these rules, you paid a real-life price, and I'm not talking about fines or free throws. You paid for these violations with your reputation, your freedom, maybe even your life. I've relied on these rules ever since—they helped save my life, and then helped me build a better one. I'm going to share them throughout this story, to pay the gift of their wisdom forward and try to help others avoid the curse built into my curriculum.

Some people say I'm lucky, and in one sense they're right. At age twenty-two, I had a random encounter with a teenager named LeBron James that changed my life. But luck is a complicated thing. We live surrounded by luck, if we know how to recognize it. Bad luck can seem good for a while; good luck might be hard to understand. My luck often arrived in disguise. It might look like a father pulling a gun on his son, or an absent mother who needed forgiveness and compassion. It might be the terrible luck of fast money or the surprising luck of a dog that doesn't bark when your life is on the line. I used to sing Kenny Rogers's "The Gambler" while playing cards or shooting dice with my friends, and I always ended with the line, *You never count your money when you're sittin' at the table / There'll be time enough for countin' when the dealing's done.*

So when it was time to negotiate my first contract, and to bet that the Phoenix Suns would give Eric Bledsoe a better deal? That was a gamble my whole life had prepared me to win.

. . .

Phoenix had actually made their first offer at the start of the previous season, but we'd said no thanks. As Bled played with the unresolved contract hanging over his head, all the other top free-agent guards got deals worth roughly forty-eight million dollars over four years—twelve million per year. The Suns came up to that number, but I held out for a fifth year on the contract. Bled felt antsy, because when you grow up not knowing where your next meal is coming from, it's hard to turn down forty-eight million dollars. I was calm, though. My life never had any room for panic. I was able to transmit some of that calm to Bled, and he trusted me, based on all the love I had poured into him since he first came into the league, the months he spent living at my house during summer workouts, the care embodied in a simple act like carrying his sneakers into the gym—all the ways my friends and I once leaned on each other to survive.

The season ended and the months passed. September arrived, training camp was approaching, and Bled was the only high-level free agent still on the market. His situation was in the news every day. I told him to leave his house in Phoenix and lay low back in Birmingham. *Don't pick up the phone when the team calls you.* Other players told him to take the latest offer. *No, Bled, trust me. We're not budging.* As other comparable players came off the board, signed to other teams, our leverage grew. By the time September ended, I knew Bled was worth a maximum contract.

The Jewish holidays were coming up, and Robert Sarver, who at the time owned the Suns, is an observant Jew. During the holidays, he doesn't do any work, not even pick up a telephone, and we knew Sarver didn't want us to get an offer from another team during the holidays when he wouldn't be able to match it.

We also represented Flip Saunders, who was coach and president of basketball operations for the Minnesota Timberwolves. Shortly before the holidays, Flip made an offhand comment in the media that Eric Bledsoe was worth a max deal.

Some people found it curious that someone we represented would make that kind of statement. Look, growing up in the streets, I never cheated in a dice game in my life. But I also knew how to roll the dice to get the numbers I needed.

Now Sarver was the one who felt antsy. The Suns came up to

five years and sixty million dollars, then sixty-five. Finally they offered five years and seventy million—fourteen million dollars per year.

The next day, Bled signed the biggest contract of any restricted free agent that off-season.

That was the first real money Klutch ever made. It sent a message to the entire NBA and laid the foundation for where I stand today. If I had botched that deal, there would be no Klutch Sports Group, which now represents more than one hundred and fifty athletes, coaches, and executives, with three billion dollars in total contracts. But we made our luck—we rolled the dice and won.

. . .

Those who call me lucky don't realize what kind of assembly line I was built on, which is understandable because I've never felt safe enough to reveal it until now. My first stroke of luck was being born into a life that forced me to be focused and prepared. Luck was learning how to recognize friendship, loyalty, love, and justice, and how to cultivate those values in life and business. Learning how to confront systems of power and not flinch, to walk on a razor's edge and never fall. Most importantly, I was lucky to learn from real Gs how to have a purpose and mission that can make a difference in people's lives, and that maybe, someday, can change the world.

You want to call me lucky? OK, bet. I was lucky from the very beginning.

# PART I

# PEACHES AND BIG RICH

RULE

**Take Care of Your People.**

# R&J CONFECTIONARY

My story begins in 1978, with a young woman walking toward the corner of 125th Street and Edmonton Avenue. She's recently arrived in Cleveland from St. Louis, looking for a fresh start at age twenty-four. A beauty with chocolate skin, a body shaped like a Coke bottle, a walk that's impossible to ignore, and a taste for the kind of street life her new city is known for. Her name is Minerva Norine Martin.

There's a store on the corner, and Minerva opens the door. She loves to dress, so she's probably wearing a skirt and some pumps, a couple rings on her fingers, with her trademark dyed streak of blond in the front of her straightened hair. The small, narrow store is clean and well stocked. It has coolers with eggs, milk, cheese, soda, and beer. Shelves with candy, bread, chips, cereal, and baking

soda. Cigarettes behind the counter. Some video games, big con-
soles almost as tall as the coolers, like Defender or Pac-Man. A
coin-operated pay phone is attached to the wall.

A man wearing a dress shirt and pleated slacks stands behind
the counter. He worked his tail off to get there: Served in the army
in Korea, sweated in a factory that made stamping machines, drove
a jitney car, installed roofs, took some college courses in business
administration, ran numbers, and had all kinds of other side hustles. It took him fifteen years to save up to buy the store's building
for twenty-five thousand dollars cash, which back then was major
paper. The man has a natural mind for business, for what people
need and how to sell it to them, whether that's milk on credit or
Acapulco Gold weed. Now he's thirty-three years old and a pillar
of the neighborhood as the owner of R&J Confectionary. The *J*
comes from the name of his wife, Justine. The *R* stands for
Richard—Richard Paul.

Richard takes stock of Minerva. He knows everybody in the
neighborhood and everybody knows him, but this is something
new.

"How you doing, sweetheart," Richard says. "How can I help
you?"

"I'm fine, thank you. Y'all got Newports?"

"For sure, baby. I never seen you around here before, where
you from?"

"St. Louis. We just moved in down the street."

"Welcome to the neighborhood. I'm here 24/7/365 for the

most part, baby. We got an after-hours thing upstairs starting at ten, bring whoever you want. Just ask for Rich, you won't have no problems. So what's your name?"

Their eyes lock. My future mother answers:

"Peaches."

. . .

That's what everybody called her: Peaches. Wasn't much soft or sweet about her, though. My mom was a firecracker, the center of attention in every room, always ready to set the party off. She grew up in St. Louis, the fifth of eleven children born to Mickey and Ruth Martin. In a family that big you had to go for yours, so my mom learned at an early age to be aggressive. If she wanted something and none of her brothers or sisters could legitimately claim it, she'd grab on to it like a pit bull. But she was a giver, too, and loved her family to death. She enjoyed taking care of her younger siblings, so she learned early how to cook amazing meals for them. When she got older, it was nothing for her to whip up a whole Sunday dinner on a random Tuesday. She worked jobs from fast-food restaurants to nursing homes and always had something moving on the side. She sold clothes or shoes that she obtained from different places—don't leave your winter coat at her house, it might end up in a yard sale that spring. She'd buy a half dozen bottles of liquor, mark them up a couple dollars, and pocket the difference. She'd bake cakes and pies and sell them up and down the street, or cook up a bunch of food, drop it into Styrofoam containers, and roll through the local bar telling people, "C'mere and give me seven dollars for this fish dinner." Pot roast, cabbage, macaroni and cheese, she could cook it all. When it came to that hustle, that grind to get money? Peaches was about that work.

She was also about those streets.

My mother liked attention. In a family of eleven kids, twelve if you count her extra stepbrother, attention was in short supply. She found it out partying. My mom started popping pills when she was thirteen years old, what they called "blues," which were like Xanax or Valium. There was a lot of weed around, too. This was the late 1960s into the early '70s and heroin was starting to hit big, but my mom was scared of needles so she didn't get into that. Her boyfriend Ralph did, though. They had two children together: my sister Brandie, who was born in 1975, when my mom was twenty years old, and my brother James, who was born in 1977.

Everybody calls my brother Meco (rhymes with "free throw"). After Meco was born, my grandfather got a job at a factory in Cleveland. He moved there, my grandmother followed him soon after, and then they broke up. Things got rough for my mom in St. Louis, with two kids whose father was addicted to heroin, so my mother brought Brandie and Meco to Cleveland, and they moved into my grandmother's house at 12617 Edmonton Avenue.

That house was half a block from Richard Paul's store.

Actually, R&J Confectionary was way more than a store. Richard Paul was the type of person who liked to take care of every-body, so R&J was also a credit union, food pantry, taxi stand, community center, and more. Parents knew their kids were safe there buying penny candy and dropping quarters into the Donkey Kong game. You could get some bread and eggs a couple days before your paycheck arrived. This was before cellphones, and guys who got locked up would use their one call from jail to ring the store pay phone and tell my dad to tell their people to bail them out. R&J Confectionary was a neighborhood institution, and Richard Paul was a caretaker of the community.

Richard took such good care of Peaches that I was born on December 16, 1980. He insisted that I have his name.

My dad was already married to Justine; they had a daughter, my sister Nicki, and they lived in a house on Ardenall Avenue in East Cleveland. But Richard Paul Sr. was not the type of man to ignore his responsibilities. He was a stand-up guy, and whatever he did, he owned it. He was always the fullest of full-time fathers to me. A few years after I was born, when Brandie and Meco's father died, Richard assumed the responsibility of raising them, too. They call him Dad to this day.

When I was a baby, Dad got my mom a place on Woodworth, not far from his house. At this time, Cleveland as a city was close to rock bottom. Once upon a time, in the late 1800s, the city was a center of American industry, the place where John D. Rockefeller built his Standard Oil empire back when Euclid Avenue was known as "Millionaires' Row." We became a factory town with strong labor unions, plenty of good working-class jobs, and a thriving Black community filled with bars, restaurants, and chitlin circuit clubs—105th Street was our version of the famed 125th in Harlem. But as the city moved through the 1970s, a lot of the machines, steel, and cars we manufactured became obsolete, or could be made cheaper in other countries. Businesses and residents left for the suburbs. Dad used to work in the Addressograph factory, which manufactured devices that stamped addresses on paper, using ink and rubber letters. That was a recipe for bankruptcy. As the jobs dried up, neighborhoods got run-down and houses were abandoned. Legal ways to make money became harder to find. People needed to survive, so crime increased.

All of this happened just in time for the arrival of crack cocaine.

A lot has been said about how crack devastated the Black community, but I'm here to testify that unless you lived through it, you really don't know. Crack had a destructive power that was unique in the history of narcotics. It was worse than the pills my mom popped, because the high was more intense but shorter in duration. It was worse than heroin, because it hyped you up instead of nodding you off. And crack smokers needed their hit so frequently, the sheer amount of product that was moving flooded the streets with cash, more than the hood had ever seen before. All that money flowing through the neighborhood increased the levels of violence in the city. So in addition to our people getting hooked on this horrific substance during the 1980s, young Black males started killing each other at an unprecedented rate.

When I was much older, I started to understand that while crack hurt a lot of people of all races, Black folks got the worst of the damage—and it was no accident. At the very least, the police and the government knew what was happening and looked the other way. There's a lot of evidence that the CIA allowed drug smugglers to sell huge amounts of cocaine in Black neighborhoods. Why would the government do that? Because America was backing the smugglers' wars against Communists in Central America. Don't forget that Congress is supposed to approve all spending by the United States government, so these CIA activities were highly illegal. But nobody cared, because crack was primarily killing Black people in the ghetto. This actually happened, it's documented, even though a lot of powerful people have tried to discredit the evidence or cover it up. I encourage you to find out more information for yourself.

Let me take it a step further, though. I believe that on some occasions, guns were deliberately placed in Black neighborhoods, because certain factions of local police and federal law enforcement wanted us to kill ourselves. People in my city talk about the time some kids were walking along train tracks, as young people sometimes do, and came across a freight car just sitting there. When they looked inside, they found crates full of guns. People in other cities reported similar experiences. Think about it: All these drugs and guns ended up in Black neighborhoods, but we didn't own no trains, no boats, no planes—Black folks didn't own none of that. That kind of trafficking doesn't happen without the knowledge or sometimes participation of larger forces.

Images of the epidemic created a picture in the mainstream American imagination of Black people as addicts, criminals, and drug dealers. Whenever they talked about crack on television or in the newspaper, it seemed like only Black people were involved. Did you know that Black people and white people both use and sell drugs at the same rate? But most people still think we are the main perpetrators, because of the false narrative that we were responsible for the explosion of crack cocaine in this country. Like we could fly down to South America and bring back kilos on demand.

But all of this was way over my head back in the 1980s. I was just a little kid wondering why his mama didn't come home. I don't mean for one night, I mean Mom didn't come home for days. Brandie took care of me and Meco, she fed us and made sure we were clean. A lot of times it was just the three of us, nobody older than ten or eleven, by ourselves for more than a week at a time.

Now, when Peaches did come home, the house best be clean when she walked in the door, and your homework done. When she was home, she pulled it together and became a good mother. I loved and respected her. Her hygiene was impeccable and whatever place she lived in was immaculate. Many mornings I woke up to the smell of Pine-Sol, bleach, and bacon, as she cleaned, cooked, and danced to the O'Jays on the stereo. Ain't no dishes in the sink. When the trash got halfway full you better take it out, and when your bath was done you better wash that dirty ring off the tub. When Mom was home, she was recharging her battery. She was getting back to the essence of the real her, and that essence was beautiful.

Then she'd leave. First she disappeared for a couple hours, then a couple days. Eventually it became weeks. When she was using we had to fend for ourselves. This is why I feel that I never got a chance to be a kid. Crack was so powerful it decimated my mother's love and expedited my adolescence. I had to grow from a cub to a young wolf right away.

From an extremely young age, I'm talking four or five years old, I was aware of my mother's addiction. I remember finding one of those velvet Crown Royal bags with drug paraphernalia in it. I remember the strange smells coming from her room. I remember hearing my grandma talking to my aunts about something being wrong with Peaches. I heard conversations I definitely shouldn't have heard. My mom's addiction and all the associated problems became normal to me. I had no idea my life was profoundly fucked up.

My dad did the best he could to make sure we were OK. As unapologetic as he was about having a child out of wedlock, he couldn't move me into his house full-time. The house was small, and his wife's mother lived with them, too. But more than that, it would have been pushing it too far with Justine to bring the child of a girlfriend to live there. I spent the night at their house once in a while, and Justine always received me with kindness. Maybe she was hiding her anger about the situation when I was around, but I never felt any animosity. Still, I couldn't live with them. Dad understood how far he could go. Which was pretty far—he paid Peaches's rent, bought us groceries, and gave us spending money. Most importantly, he gave us his love and his time.

But as anyone who has tried to help addicts knows, you can't rely on them to do normal things. So in 1985, when I was five years old, my father brought my mom, Brandie, Meco, and me to live in an apartment above his store.

My education was about to begin.

RULE

**Other People Are
Your Business.**

## 2

# NO "I LOVE YOUS"

Dad unlocked the door of R&J Confectionary at six every morning. Some days I opened the store with him and worked until about eight, when he saw me off to school. After school I came right back to work at the store—running the cash register and the lottery machine, stocking shelves, not to mention playing video games, eating Doritos, and drinking Hawaiian Punch. The store was my favorite place in the world.

I know what you're thinking: *How can a six- or seven-year-old boy run a cash register?* Well, I knew how to count, and I had been watching my dad on the register for as long as I could remember. Making change was just addition and subtraction to a hundred. The register was basically a calculator. Easy.

A few minutes after the store opened each morning, the doughnut man arrived, like clockwork. Jack Frost Donuts on St. Clair Avenue made every batch from scratch, and our customers fiended for them so hard they were almost like crack. Almost. Then the stacks of newspapers got dropped off, first the *Plain Dealer,* then the *Call and Post*. Different customers bought either paper for different reasons. The *Call and Post* was Black-owned-and-operated, so folks felt that it gave you the real. The *Plain Dealer* was the white paper that gave you what the big shots who ran the city wanted you to think. The number runners used figures from the *Call and Post* to set their bets, not the *Plain Dealer*.

The morning rush included people from all walks of life. You had the working folks headed to their jobs, a mix of blue-collar people and then folks like schoolteachers or office workers. You had the dope boys who had been on the streets all night, plus the crackheads and the "strawberries," the women who prostituted themselves to buy drugs. A drug dealer might be standing next to a guy in a suit and tie, both of them making sure to get a doughnut before they all disappeared.

Then you had tons of kids on their way to school. The high schoolers came first, a flow of teenagers from freshmen to seniors. There were distinct differences between the grades. Some of the seniors had cars, they might be with their girlfriends, or might not even be going to school. Seniors were laid-back compared with the freshmen, who were still playful and wide-eyed, just excited to be in high school. Then the younger students from middle and elementary school came in with their parents. At its peak we might have twenty kids packed into the store, making their rounds: Grab a doughnut or a twist and a Big Hug juice, then pull up to the glass counter that had all the candy inside. A girl might say, "Lemme get five Super Bubbles and a Black Cow. How much I got left?" Twenty cents. "OK, then I'll take two watermelon Jolly Ranchers and the rest in peppermints." Now picture a line of twenty kids jostling and talking in the store's small space. Dad had a serious demeanor but was always friendly and welcoming. "These kids keep me paid," he used to say. "Penny candy puts food on our table." I had a vicious sweet tooth myself, well into adulthood.

If it was warm outside, some boys played football in the street in front of the store until the school bus came. Other boys went outside and sold dope before going to school. Some kids stayed in the store to play video games. My dad let kids hang out in the store until 7:35 A.M., and then they had to go. If they didn't get off the video game, he'd unplug it, he didn't care if they were about to beat the game, had money riding on it, or whatever. He'd say, "You're not going to be loitering in here during school hours. That's not going to happen."

Dad grew up with both of his parents in housing projects near 55th Street and Central Avenue, before moving to Scottwood off of Lakeview Road. As a young man he moved in the same circles as George Forbes, who became a city councilman, and Don King, who became one of the greatest boxing promoters of all time. My dad's most notable acquaintance, though, was Carl Stokes, who in 1967 was elected mayor of Cleveland—the first Black mayor of a major, predominantly white American city. When I was a kid, Stokes used to stop in the store sometimes and chop it up with my dad.

After high school, like most Black men in the city, Dad either had to get a job or join the armed forces. College wasn't a realistic option then for kids from the projects. So he did some time in the service and then started saving up money to buy the store building, because he was tired of getting laid off from this or that factory and wanted to go into business for himself. What put him over the top for purchasing the property was when he hit a number. He won a nice stack of cash and used that to buy the building. A Black man couldn't save up twenty-five thousand dollars working the type of low-wage jobs that were available to us in the 1970s, and no bank was going to lend a Black man with a high school education that much money.

Dad was short and slim, with a well-trimmed mustache, soft hair, and a medium-brown complexion. He dressed nicely for the store every day: slacks, a collared shirt, sometimes a three-piece suit. Jeans were a foreign object to him—"that's what a mechanic wears," he said. He always wore spectator or cap-toe dress shoes, "leather or lizard," which means he had some gators. Occasionally, toward the end of the week, he'd sport a pinky ring with his initials on it. He drove a blue Cadillac Coupe DeVille with a soft top.

The same way I overheard conversations about my mother's drug problems and understood them at a young age, I listened to my dad interacting with people and came to understand how he became successful and admired. Dad was the type of guy that everybody wanted to know, five-foot-seven-inches tall with a six-foot-five reputation. He was a charmer, with a great sense of humor, but could instantly flip the switch if something went sideways, which was always a possibility in our neighborhood. From my post behind the counter, I observed that selling lots of food, beer, and cigarettes was just the surface level of my father's success. The bedrock of the business was the way he treated all the people he interacted with and their exchange of respect, no matter their station in life or status. A lot of people in the neighborhood called him "The Godfather."

Dad had a little TV behind the counter, next to a water jug he put five dollars into every day to save up for his annual trip to Las Vegas. We spent a lot of quiet time in the store together, just the two of us, and he used those moments to talk to me, delivering lessons about life. At the end of each conversation he'd say, "I'm not going to be here forever, son. When I'm gone, you got to know these things." Some lessons were direct and simple, like how to spot a dope fiend—they're jittery and don't make a lot of eye contact. Others were more philosophical. On some days we'd drive to the candy wholesaler on 133rd in East Cleveland and he would send me inside by myself with three hundred dollars cash to buy Now and Laters, Jolly Ranchers, and everything else we needed. I liked orange Now and Laters myself, but I'd already learned from watching my dad that what I liked didn't matter. I had to buy the flavors that would sell best in the store: tropical punch, pineapple, and watermelon. Forget about grape, none of our customers liked those. When we got back to the store and he looked at what I'd bought, Dad nodded with approval: "That's how it's done, Lil Bear. Ain't nobody got money to be wasting on stuff people don't want."

Dad had a friend who was like a brother, my Uncle Joe, and he helped run the store. Sometimes Uncle Joe watched the register while my dad walked me to Captain Arthur Roth Elementary School, which was a block up 125th on Woodside Avenue. On the way to school my dad always talked to me about my classes, but he was a big sports fan, too. We discussed what the Cleveland Browns were doing on the football field, how many points Michael Jordan had scored last night, or who Mike Tyson was going to knock out next. I don't remember the exact words of those talks, but I remember the feeling. As we traded thoughts and ideas, I felt my father's attention like a warm spotlight. I always knew there was someone in the world who cared about what I was doing, what I thought, who I was becoming—that feeling is still what defines love to me. It's interesting how Black men get stereotyped as not taking care of their children because a lot of us are not married to the mother of our kids. But not being married doesn't mean those fathers don't care for their children. Not just financially, but in that way that my father showed his love: genuine, persistent time and attention. In fact, data shows that Black men, including fathers who don't live full-time with their children, spend as much or more time raising those children as other fathers. My dad was one of many unheralded Black dads who were deeply involved in the lives of their children.

By this time my father was no longer selling Acapulco Gold. That was something he had to do to buy the building and open his store, but my dad was never a drug dealer in spirit. He didn't have a criminal mindset. He was an entrepreneur, a hustler, someone who always knew the correct next move. He wanted to control his own financial destiny, not depend on someone else for a job. Marijuana had been one of his many revenue streams, and after he opened the store he no longer needed to take that risk. Also, by then the drug game had become dominated by crack, which my dad wanted no part of. By the time I lived above his store, he was a legitimate businessman.

Well, mostly legit.

A little ways down from the entrance to the store was another door. Inside that door was a staircase. At the top of the stairs was another door that opened into a large space, like a hallway or vestibule. To the left was the apartment where I lived with Mom, Brandie, and Meco. To the right was an apartment where Uncle Joe lived. And when night fell, Uncle Joe's crib turned into an after-hours spot.

Call it a speakeasy, a juke joint, or whatever, but it was definitely popping. Most of the customers were people from the neighborhood who got off the late shift and wanted to relax and have a drink before going home. It had a makeshift bar and a card table. Sometimes people shot dice up against the wall. I wasn't in there a whole lot when it was in full effect, being so young at the time, but I heard the music playing and saw grown folks coming and going. From my perspective, it didn't seem strange at all. It was just another part of Dad's business.

Our apartment had two bedrooms, a living room with a little balcony looking out over the street, a kitchen, and one bathroom. My mom slept in one bedroom, and there were twin beds in the other. Brandie slept in one twin bed, and I shared the other with Meco. He slept with his head at the top of the bed, and my head was at the bottom. Uncle Joe took over at the store every day from two o'clock until it closed at seven-thirty, after the lottery numbers came out. My dad would come upstairs with us for a few hours, then go to the house he shared with his wife and daughter. But sometimes he spent the night with us.

I saw flashes of what a normal life could be during those times in our home above the store. My mom playing music while she cooked, dancing in the kitchen and stirring her pots to the Isley Brothers, the O'Jays, Bobby Womack, Teddy Pendergrass, Anita Baker, Tina Turner, Luther Vandross, the Spinners, Diana Ross, and the Temptations. That's where my love of music comes from: the joy of watching Mom dancing and singing along to her favorites. She loved the romantic balladeers, but Dad's favorite was "Practice What You Preach" by Barry White, a song about love and accountability. In those years she would sometimes take us out to eat at Red Lobster or a Japanese hibachi restaurant called the Samurai House. She ordered mai tais and let me taste them. I have great memories of those times when Mom was home with us and doing well.

In between those happy moments, a different version of my mother emerged, a tough, hardcore woman I barely recognized as the same person. Just as our home environment brought out the singing, dancing, cooking, enterprising mother I loved, the streets brought out her survival instincts. Her motto was "I wish a nigga would." If someone came at her wrong in the street, she'd pull a knife or hit them upside the head with a bat. I never saw her do that, but word got around. Mom could definitely handle herself.

My parents' toughness wasn't just for the streets. I remember one night my mom made beans for dinner. I hated beans, and for some reason that was the night six-year-old me decided to draw the line: *No beans.* I made my feelings clear and I thought Mom was the one I would have to go up against. I braced for her to start yelling. But then all of sudden I felt myself lifted up out of my chair. Dad had my skinny arm gripped in one hand and his belt in the other. This was an unexpected development, because Meco was the one who got whoopings, not me. My dad got to swinging that belt and I danced like a puppet on a string trying to avoid the blows. Mom just looked at us with a stone-faced expression. Dad kept saying, "You better sit down and eat those beans!" but I wouldn't sit down. "Nobody's leaving this table until you eat those beans!" Meco said later that he wanted to eat the beans for me, that's how hard Dad swung his belt. But for some reason, I still refused. The whooping ended, and I didn't eat the beans.

We felt love but didn't get many "I love yous" growing up. Mom was consumed with fighting her problems, and Dad's love came in the form of discipline, pushing, reprimanding, attention, and expectation. Dad didn't feel he could broadcast his love in ways that hinted at his own vulnerability, because that could get you killed in our neighborhood. He was preparing us to survive in an unforgiving environment. Like Jay-Z says in his record "Heart of the City," there's no love when you're in the jungle, man. Ain't no love in those streets. At least not the kind you could just declare openly, the kind of love that exists in pretty words. Instead, we found love in hard places, through adversity, through struggle. I found love in my father's tough lessons. And I found it through the bond I developed with other guys as we fought through the pain of our lives. Everybody's pain was different and came from a different source, but I was pretty clear on the roots of my own: watching my mother disappear.

No "I love yous" is a lesson I carry today, even in business—I know that words and cheap sentiment have no value. I don't expect anything from anybody. I don't expect other agents or the media to praise me, I don't expect professional sports teams to care about me or my guys. Even when it comes to my clients, as much as I love my guys, the main way I care for them is by telling them the truth. This doesn't always go down easily—most pro athletes are surrounded by people who tell them every day how great they are. Some athletes get tired of hearing me tell them the truth. At some point, they buck. But it's the only way I know to show real care—by paying attention and telling the truth. In the end, it's the only kind of love that matters.

I wonder what her life's trajectory would have been if my mom had access to a professional environment. Peaches had so much entrepreneurial talent and toughness and drive, what might have happened if she had avoided drugs and worked at a steel company, or in the office at Ford or GM? What if she'd landed a job at the management company IMG, which started in Cleveland? Could my mom have worked her way up into the executive ranks, maybe earned bonuses or equity? Could my father have started a chain of grocery stores or another major business? What could my parents' talents have produced under different circumstances?

I can get lost in that kind of speculation now, but back then, all I knew was the life I had. Everything I learned, I learned at that store, and it all seemed perfectly normal to me—even when Brandie and I heard banging at the back door of the store in the dead of winter and found a guy there doubled over, red blood soaking into the white snow. It seemed normal to take a brown slip of paper and write down the cost of a dozen eggs with the customer's name on it, put that slip in the far side of the cash register, then trade the slip for cash on payday. There were lessons in everything.

There was a lot I didn't learn, too. The people around me

couldn't teach me about higher education, business infrastructure, macroeconomics, personal finance, or how to build a career. How do you climb the corporate ladder? What does security look like? What is a good life? No one was modeling that for me. My models were Black people in the ghetto who had no choice but to find a way out of a dead-end situation. My models were hustlers.

In popular street terminology, "hustler" usually means drug dealer. My definition is a little more expansive. I define a hustler as someone who is never complacent, always thinking two steps ahead of everyone else. Someone who can manage the transitions. If things turn upside down, a hustler adapts to being upside down without missing a step. They never get stuck in a situation, and always understand what move to make in order to accomplish their goals. Both of my parents were hustlers, and that's where my education began. It's a real-world education that comes with a lot of risk, and not every hustler succeeds, that's for sure, but I wouldn't be where I am today without it.

Here's something else about hustlers: They rarely go broke.

One day after school I was in the store with my dad, playing Defender or whatever video game we had in the store at the time. Things were slow and the store was empty.

"Come over here for a minute, Lil Bear," my dad said. He was in the small room at the back of the store that we used for storage.

Dad squatted next to a pillowcase laid out on the floor, holding something in his fist.

"Sometimes in life you might get laid off from work, or something else might go wrong and you find yourself without a job," he said. "If that happens, a man needs another way to support himself and his family. I'm gonna show you how you can always make money if you need it. These right here are the tools to get you through."

My father shook his fist, cocked it back, then swung it down and opened it. Out tumbled two tiny, magical cubes.

When those dice hit the floor, everything changed.

RULE

**Leave Nothing to Chance.**

# 3

# THE BLOCK

First my dad showed me how to play craps: If you throw a seven or eleven on the first roll, you win. If you throw two, three, or twelve on the first roll, you lose. Once you roll any other number—four, five, six, eight, nine, ten—you have to roll that number again to win. While you're trying to match that number, if you roll seven or eleven, you lose. Those are the basics.

Then Dad pulled some money out of his pocket and showed me how to bet. The bills got my attention. He explained that not only could I bet on myself when I was rolling the dice, but I could bet on someone else when it was their turn. I didn't even have to be in the game to win—or lose. There were any number of ways to make or lose money on this game, just from those two little dice. That same day, Dad also showed me how to play a gambling card game called tunk. That was fun, but there was something about the dice that drew me in.

I was about six years old.

The rules were simple, winning was hard. Dad carefully watched me practice and was very precise with his instructions. "No, Lil Bear, you can't just throw the dice crazy like that. There's a certain way to do it. Throw them like *this*." And they tumbled softly out of his fist onto the pillowcase.

As time went on, I realized that Dad did everything consciously. Nothing was accidental, impulsive, or emotional. He always moved with intention. He was a gambler who left nothing to chance.

. . .

In 1987, we moved from above the store back to my grandma's place up the block on Edmonton. My grandma Ruth Martin worked as a receptionist at the vocational center on 55th and Cedar. The only other person living in the house besides us was my mother's sister, Aunt San, who had Down's syndrome. Our first-floor unit only had two bedrooms, so when we moved in, Grandma Ruth bought a couch that let out into a bed, and she slept in the living room. I either slept on the floor or in the same bed as my brother or sister.

My whole world was Edmonton Avenue, which is four blocks long. Edmonton is located within a neighborhood known as Glenville, and Glenville is part of the larger East Side of Cleveland. But none of the larger world was apparent to me. All I could see was the block.

Edmonton consisted of older, two-story wood-frame houses, sometimes divided into smaller units, with porches outside both the first and second floors. Edmonton also had a deeper layer that outsiders might not notice: a network of alleys, yards, metal fences, and open spaces where us kids roamed. The four blocks run east to west starting at 131st Street. Each block had a different weight to it. The 131st Street side was nicer and more calm; nobody hustled over there. There were mostly older families on those streets, living in houses with fences that enclosed clean front yards. Moving west, things got more hectic as you approached my grandmother's house, Number 12617. Past my grandmother's house was Dad's store on the corner of 125th Street, which was a central location for the neighborhood. That's where things got wild. There was so much traffic and action, you never knew what might happen. The pay phone outside the store drew a lot of activity. It seemed like half the neighborhood had the number memorized: 249-0219. The phone rang at all hours with callers looking for somebody. Past the store was the final block of Edmonton, which ended at Eddy Road, a series of empty lots with an apartment building at the end. The Eddy Road side was rough and rugged. It had badder kids—Tommy, Big Ju, Earl, Ernie, the Berrys, the Roses. It was also way more fun. I spent a lot of time at that end because my friend Marty from kindergarten lived there, and his mom ran with Peaches.

Right next to Marty's apartment building was the Dust Bowl, a dirt field where we played every sport. So many feet had run over and slid on and tramped down the dirt, no grass ever grew on it. We had two rollaway basketball hoops for playing full court. We also nailed a milk crate to a pole, which is where I developed my jumper. My shot had to be dead-on because the pole had no backboard, just a naked crate up there. We played football and baseball, too. There was a home plate in the ground right under the hoop, so when you drove the lane playing basketball you had to be careful not to trip on the plate. Everybody knew not to wear anything white to the Dust Bowl, because if you fell once, you ruined your clothes. The atmosphere was very competitive, it was a known spot in the neighborhood. Putting in work at the Dust Bowl solidified your reputation as an athlete.

Most of the families on the block knew each other. I was a responsible kid, and my mom was not always around to supervise, so I had a lot of leeway to venture into the nooks and crannies of our street, and to travel back and forth between Marty's house, the store, and my grandma's house.

Dad made sure I always had spending money, and I started using those funds to shoot dice with my little friends. We'd go around back of the store or find an alley and get to it. I sharpened my game at family reunions and barbecues where a dice game always seemed to break out in the yard or the basement. That unmistakable circle would form, and you could tell just from guys' posture what was going down. My eyes would light up, and Dad would hand me twenty dollars and say, "Go ahead and see what you can do."

You know how little kids have a favorite stuffed animal, a teddy bear they carry around with them, that they love because it makes them feel safe and comfortable? The dice were my teddy bear. Right from the start, I had a knack for winning. The numbers you roll are random, but there are lots of factors that influence winning and losing. My dad taught me all the combinations, which means what bets to make depending on what points are rolled and what had just happened in the game. Like, if the shooter is trying to hit a four, bet against him, because there are only two number combinations that add up to four. If he's trying to hit an eight, bet with him, because there are three combinations. But all those probabilities go out the window sometimes based on the vibe and whether the dude is hot. I soaked up all the information I could from Dad and almost always won more than I lost, to the point where it felt like I had a gift. I'm seven years old coming back to the store from a dice game with a bunch of crumpled one-dollar bills, a couple fives, maybe thirty dollars total. Soon, I'm bringing home tens and twenties. Then one day after school a kid started bragging about how nice he was at the Street Fighter video game.

"Oh word?" I said. "You can't beat me though. How much you wanna bet right now?"

"Bet you a dollar."

"A dollar? A dollar ain't shit." That may sound crazy for a seven-year-old to say, but that's how I heard people cussing around me every day. Plus, I was feeling myself. I slapped a five-dollar bill on the console and said, "If you that good, put some real money up."

The kid said, "Bet."

Now I had diversified income streams: dice and video games. Tunk, too. The first time I showed Dad my little bankroll, his eyebrows shot up.

"OK boy, that's how you get down. Since you serious with this, let me explain a couple things to you.

"The hand is quicker than the eye. Guys can deal from the bottom of the deck and you'll never know.

"Be careful. Know the robbers, know the jackers, know the schemers.

"Don't pull out a roll of money in front of people. Peel off what you need and only let them see that. Understand that the closest person to you will knock your head off for that roll.

"And never cheat," my father told me. "Because that will get you killed."

RULE

**Iron Your Clothes.**

# 4

## LITTLE RICH

n addition to dice, I discovered another tool of survival in those early days: the iron.

That's right, a regular household iron, used to press the wrinkles out of clothes. In my young hands, the iron was a weapon I could use to keep chaos and neglect from taking me under. The iron was an instrument of salvation.

As least that's how I think about it now. I didn't see it that way at the time. All I knew was that I wanted—I needed—to look good, to have nice clothes, to have people notice me for something positive. Both of my parents were always on point with their outfits, so I had them as models of how to present myself, but my sister Brandie is the one who taught me how to be a great ironer. Unlike my parents, Brandie was with me every morning when it was time

to get dressed. She had a great eye for fashion and, most importantly, she knew how to shop on our limited budget. Starting when
Brandie was twelve or thirteen years old, she took me and Meco on
the ninety-minute city bus ride to the Euclid Square Mall, where
she'd spend her babysitting money on clothes and buy us a little
something, too. The Euclid mall had stores like Higbee's, May
Company, Foot Locker, 5-7-9, J.Crew, and Wild Pair. Brandie was
the first person to turn me on to Polo when she bought shirts from
T.J.Maxx and Value City, where they sometimes sold irregular or
defective items below price, and fixed them up with a stitch here or
a snip of fabric there.

I watched Brandie iron our clothes in the mornings, and was
intrigued. Brandie started to teach me how to do it for myself.
She'd hold her hand over mine as we pressed clothes. I had to stand
on a chair to reach the board, or sometimes we laid the board on
the bed. Pretty soon I was doing it for myself. The way my jeans
felt smooth and warm to the touch after I finished ironing, how my
shirt fell in a clean line from my shoulder to my waist—it just
made me feel right.

When I was about six years old, my sister Nicki, who is Dad's
daughter, bought me a Richie Rich sweater with a plastic bubble
version of the cartoon character on the front. I absolutely loved
that sweater, and for months I wore it every Wednesday. Brandie
told me not to iron plastic, so I carefully avoided Richie Rich's little
blond face. Of course the time came when I slipped up and touched
that plastic bubble with the iron and melted his head. I was so upset

you would have thought a family member died, but I kept wearing the sweater anyway, melted or not.

I studied the outfits of older guys who had money—my uncles, dope boys, pimps, players—not only for what they wore, but how they wore it. Uncle Lance wore his sneakers all the way unlaced, but his shoe stayed magically attached to his foot. Slim Black up the block wore his hat tilted at a precise angle that even the wind couldn't shift. One of my brother's friends, a dude on our block named Mike Ivey, alternated New Balance or Adidas soccer shoes called Sambas with the Nikes everybody else wore. The variety made him stand out. I absorbed all these details of originality and presentation.

My father bought Brandie, Meco, and me what we needed and most of what we asked for, so I could compete. At Captain Arthur Roth Elementary, where I went to school from kindergarten through third grade, I started the Nike Crew. You had to wear all-Nike to be down. I had the top and bottom sweats and the Cortez sneakers. When I saw the dope boys wearing Lotto and Fila and Diadora sneakers, I got those, too. It was a weird juxtaposition of being broke and, in my mind, thinking I was wealthy because I had fly clothes. That happens in the ghetto because we're cut off from the wider world, so we think we've reached the top when we're barely above water. But mostly, the praise I got for looking fresh helped soothe the pain of my mom's absence.

For my third-grade graduation I wore an all-white tuxedo, with tails, and an electric blue cummerbund. Plus, Dad rented a limo.

But my name really started to ring out for being well dressed when I was nine years old and bought the Air Jordan 4 sneakers out of the Sears catalog. First they came out in powder blue with gray and white accents, then in white and black with the specks on them, then in all black. When I got my hands on those Jordan 4s, I was so eager to get to school the next day, I could barely sleep. The D.O.C. song "The Formula" had just dropped, and my Uncle Lance played it all the time at Grandma's house on Edmonton. In my mind I saw myself wearing the 4s and stepping down the block to that Dr. Dre beat with the Marvin Gaye sample. I had the formula for a dope outfit, for sure.

That morning, I turned the iron all the way up to the highest setting and got to work. I owned three pairs of jeans but only two good ones; the black stonewashed pair went perfectly with my new sneakers. When I could see the heat coming off the iron I started putting the creases in my jeans. I had to start from the bottom hem and iron up, not move from the waist down. That way, I could align the leg seams with the crease. When you did it properly, the seam formed a subtle ridge down the side of the pants, parallel to the crease. Anything off-line was no good. Any trace of a double crease was completely unacceptable. A double crease happened when you messed up your line and had to go back to make another one, which ended up looking like two creases close together on the front of the pants. No way I was walking outside the house with a double crease. I used the steam button on the iron to remove stubborn wrinkles, but my main ally was Niagara spray starch in the green can. I didn't go too heavy with the starch, though, because that would mess with the drape and flow of the fabric.

Attention to detail still defines my life. When you practice doing little things the right way, it helps the big things fall into place.

After I got done ironing, it was time to focus on my sneakers. The presentation of the sneakers was very important. You couldn't just tie them any old way. I laced my Jordans to the second hole from the top, which let the tongue of the sneaker ride outside the bottom of my jeans. I wore a black belt that day; I hope it was leather, but it might have been related to that Richie Rich material. My shirt was red, with something about sports on the front. Mom bought it from Value City, so it might've been a little off. But my shirt was secondary because the Jordans were more than enough. Owning a pair of Jordans was like owning a house. I had all three pairs of the Jordan 4s. The response was everything I wanted: "There go Little Rich with the Jordans." "Little Rich stay fresh."

Over the years, I've heard a lot of negative comments from outside our community about how poor Black people spend so much money on sneakers or the latest iPhone. Here's what they don't understand: When I was a kid, everything felt surface-deep in my life. There was nothing to get to the bottom of. We were conditioned to think that getting and spending money defined success. Today, I hear people talk about "getting the bag." Very few people talk about building something that *provides* the bag. I tell the athletes and other young people I mentor to use their resources to find opportunities to build something, to believe in it, bet on it, and do everything they can to add value. The rest will come.

But all of that was beyond me as a kid. When you live in an environment that's liable to spin out of control at any moment, a fresh pair of sneakers and a sharply pressed outfit will hold you down.

RULE

**Discipline Your Approach.**

# 5

## THE BAT OR THE GAT

Late one night, about one A.M., I was lying on the floor in the living room of my Grandma Ruth's house on Edmonton, watching TV while my grandmother slept. I heard noises outside. Grandma Ruth woke up and looked outside, where she saw a shadow moving up the side of the house. She got up and went to the stove, where she always kept a pot of water on low heat, and turned up the flame. We heard somebody scrabbling around on the upstairs porch. Our landlord, Mrs. Willis, lived above us, and she kept some bicycles on the second-story porch. After about a minute, a crackhead climbed down the side of the house with a bike over his shoulder. Grandma Ruth grabbed the pot of hot water, opened the window, and doused him. He screamed, dropped the bike, and ran off. I went back to watching my show.

. . .

The first local Cleveland rap group I remember making a splash was Brothers 4 the Struggle. These dudes were hard, with an East Coast lyrical style, but their raps were filled with specific places and events in our neighborhood, using our special slang. Their songs became the soundtrack to our lives, and one in particular, "It's Over," was like our anthem. We memorized every word, and Meco and I performed it for our friends and families at cookouts and re- unions: *In the beginning I wasn't winning I was taking a beating / I produced enough juice to keep the enemy retreating . . .* Whenever I rapped that line, I felt its truth in my own life.

When I wasn't outside hustling up some money, I was at the store. I liked to sip on black coffee with sugar, like my dad drank it, and study the sports section of the *Plain Dealer*. I scrutinized those pages every day, reading all the fine print and box scores that de- scribed the details of games from every sport. Every detail mat- tered to me, down to the uniforms. I liked the Orlando Magic pinstripe uniforms and the New England Patriots three-point- stance logo. When I got to school, I could compete with anybody when it came to facts and figures about basketball, football, base- ball, even hockey.

Dad always asked me to run the lottery machine. That was a tough assignment. Mr. Smith might come in and want to play 5-1-5, dollar straight, dollar box. That's his "pick three," meaning three numbers. "Straight" means you win if the numbers come up in that order; with a "box" they can be in any order but the payout is lower. Mr. Smith's pick four might be his license plate, 4-6-4-4, two dollars straight, dollar box. I was under a lot of pressure to get all this exactly right, because Mr. Smith might have been playing these numbers for six months and they ain't hit yet—if they did hit, I'd better be sure to have recorded it right. I have to move fast, too, because there's a long line of people waiting to bet their own numbers. If Mr. Smith looks at his slip as he's walking out the door and I got one digit wrong, ain't nobody letting him cut the line—"Mothafucka, I been waiting to play my number, too!" There's a cutoff time for buying tickets, and if any of these people in line don't get their number in, they feel like they want to kill somebody. This is the situation my dad put me in at seven or eight years old. It gave me focus and calm under pressure. It also sharpened my math skills, so now in school I'm adding and multiplying numbers in my head like a human calculator. Dad knew exactly what he was doing.

He had words of wisdom or advice for everybody who came through, especially us kids. Sometimes people didn't want to hear it, but they had no choice. Dad dealt with everybody straight-up, no punches pulled, never afraid to tell you where you stood. I call him a man's man, because he always did things from a place of integrity and principle. He closely observed everyone who came in and out of the store and took note of everything going on in their lives, which was a lot because Edmonton and 125th was a hotbed of activity—legal, illegal, and everything in between. A young hustler might walk in the store and Dad would tell him how his whole life would unfold if he didn't slow down, and the dude didn't even know that my dad knew his name. "Boy, you out here doing bad things, you're either going to jail or the cemetery. Ain't no ifs, ands, or buts about it. Take your ass away from around here." There was no incentive for him to say that, other than his principles and a desire to see everyone do better. Sometimes he knew guys were too deep in the game to just stop, so he'd give them a different piece of advice: "It's all about your approach."

It's hard to understand that even in the game there are differences in how you approach it. There are ways to maintain some control and minimize harm, even if just for a little while, and ways that are sloppy, careless, and lead to quick and unnecessary suffering. It sounds obvious but it's easy to forget: Having a disciplined and thoughtful approach to your work day in and day out, especially when the work is difficult and risky, will determine your level of success. I give that same advice to my clients now. How athletes approach their jobs is crucial. Getting to the facility early, saying thank you to the people who pick up the towels or set out the food. If you're in the playoffs with idle time, will your approach be to sit around smoking hookah and scrolling through Instagram? Or will you watch film, stay on top of your diet, get proper rest so you can give your team 110 percent? I learned this by listening to all the advice I heard my dad give people as they came through the store and then watching the results. Time and time again, I saw people who didn't listen and then suffered the consequences. I've sat so many athletes down and said, "Look, if you don't change what you're doing, this is what's going to happen." Some guys listen; some don't. I have clients who would be a hundred million dollars richer if they had only changed their approach. Every day you wake up and bring yourself to the world in an undisciplined and thoughtless way is a day you put yourself closer to failure than success.

Here's another thing: Dad didn't believe in repeating himself. If he said it once, he wouldn't say it again. Some kids might be playing the video games when they should have been in school. Dad would look up from the TV he kept behind the counter and call out, "Hey! Y'all can't be in here during school hours. I can't make you go to school, but I can make you get up outta here." If they didn't stop playing, Dad would hop off his stool, walk behind the game, yank out the power cord without a word, and return to his perch behind the counter.

One time some kids he had previously told not to loiter in the store were clowning around. Maybe they were bolder than usual because Uncle Joe was working the counter and not Dad. The kids got to carrying on, ignoring Uncle Joe, acting loud and disrespectful. There was a curtain at the back of the store that opened into the stockroom. All of a sudden the curtain parted and Dad swept through. He was wearing dress slacks, no shirt, and a pistol in a holster strapped across his bare, skinny chest.

"Which one you want, the bat or the gat?" Dad barked.

Everybody knew he kept a baseball bat behind the counter. Everybody could see the gat strapped to his chest. The kids chose neither and ran out the door.

. . .

Our neighborhood was all Black. That applied to Edmonton, Glenville, and the whole East Side in general. I don't remember seeing but one or two white people living there. Everything was totally segregated, by design.

In the early 1900s, millions of Black people fled the racism of the Deep South in the Great Migration, and came to Northern cities looking for good jobs and more freedom than they could find in the racist South. To this day, if you ask most Black folks in Cleveland where their people are from, they'll name some town in the Southern black belt. My grandmother was originally from Jonesboro, Arkansas. Lots of families came from Alabama, Tennessee, Mississippi. The irony is that when our ancestors arrived in Cleveland, they still faced segregation, especially in terms of where they could live.

Before the Great Migration, Cleveland was filled with what used to be called "ethnic" white people—Hungarian, Italian, Polish, German, Irish, and other recent immigrants. As tens of thousands of Black people arrived in Cleveland, ethnic white people moved out, to suburbs like Shaker Heights, Cleveland Heights, and Euclid. Black folks were legally prohibited from living in most white neighborhoods, and when they did make it in there, sometimes their houses got bombed. That's why, by the 1950s, the East Side of Cleveland was all Black.

Next came a racist policy called "redlining," when banks and government agencies got together and decided not to make home loans in Black neighborhoods. That drove down the property values, the houses got run-down, and Black residents couldn't build up wealth through home equity. That's a major reason why the East Side became a ghetto. The same thing happened across America. Don't let anybody fool you into thinking Black neighborhoods are jacked up because we're irresponsible or criminally inclined or too lazy to work. We were systematically confined to certain areas that were then drained of wealth, jobs, and resources. In a lot of places, we still are.

. . .

There was a bus stop a short block down from the store, at 125th and Arlington. When I was about seven years old, Dad started taking me downtown on the No. 3 bus. Our destination was always the same: Public Square, where we'd buy a hot dog at a stand and then ride back home. This was my first look at the world beyond my immediate neighborhood, my first glimpse of my city's wider reality. It wasn't much.

In the mid-1980s, the city as a whole was suffering. Our population had quickly declined over the last couple of decades from a peak of almost a million to less than six hundred thousand. The steel industry was half of what it had been in the 1970s, which meant fewer jobs, a smaller tax base, and less spending in stores. People still talked about when the polluted Cuyahoga River caught on fire in 1969. The poverty rate was about 30 percent. We were the epitome of the Rust Belt. Our baseball team was terrible. The Cavaliers were mediocre and about to disappear in the shadow of Michael Jordan. The Browns broke Cleveland's heart in the AFC championship game two seasons in a row: 1986, when John Elway led the Broncos on a 98-yard last-minute touchdown drive to win the game; and 1987, when Earnest Byner fumbled the tying touchdown on the goal line. All this created a sense that a dark cloud hung over the city.

The No. 3 bus took Arlington to 123rd Street, which turned into Superior, a commercial avenue that went all the way to Public Square. The ride lasted more than an hour each way, and during that time Dad talked to me about the different blocks and streets and what they were like. If a bunch of young people got on the bus, Dad shared observations with me—that one there could be dangerous; that one is scared. When we got off at Public Square, I saw more white people than anyplace I had ever been. The buildings were big, but they weren't skyscrapers like I saw on television. The Key Tower wasn't built yet. Dad and I walked around, bought our hot dog, and then rode back home. I loved those rides because it was time spent with my dad. No hot dog has ever tasted better than the ones I ate in Public Square. But on another level, I wondered: *Is this the best there is?*

Growing up in Cleveland wasn't like living in Harlem, where you could walk twenty minutes and be at Central Park or the Museum of Natural History or the luxuries of Fifth Avenue. We had no Empire State Building, no Sears Tower like Chicago, no Pacific Ocean like Los Angeles, no White House like Washington, DC. All you could see in Cleveland was more Cleveland. The city back then could kill your ambitions in the crib. The first obstacle that many of us encountered in Cleveland was the biggest one we'd ever face: To envision a better life, your imagination had to be extraordinary. You had to chase something you never saw with your own eyes.

Looking out the window of the No. 3 bus, I didn't know what I was searching for. But I could feel dreams stirring inside of me. I was definitely searching for *something*.

# PART II

# CHAOS
# AT THE
# DOOR

RULE

**Build an Ecosystem
of Empathy.**

## 6

# A SOULLESS HOOD

On a sunny afternoon, I left the store to go to my friend Keith's house. He lived next to the vacant lot on Edmonton that was across the street from the store. I had just crossed Edmonton when I heard a bunch of arguing and cussing. I turned and saw people running up and down the driveway across the street from Keith's. That was the house where a family of gangsters and dope dealers lived. The family had five brothers: Mike, Slim Black, Onnie, Deron, and Tommy. I was halfway across the vacant lot when I saw Mike run up to the front of the store, open the door, and yell inside:

"Big Rich, gimme your pistol!"

The next thing I heard was *BOW!* A huge gunshot from farther down the block.

I was caught in no-man's-land and had to make a quick decision. Keith's house was the closest safe haven, so I sprinted toward his bushes, dove over them into his yard, and crawled up onto his porch. Keith was lying flat on the porch, too, trying to see what was going on. Together we peered out at the gunfight unfolding on Edmonton Avenue.

A guy called Stack lived about fifteen houses down from Keith, toward 131st Street. He came from a normal family, with two parents who worked. They weren't gangsters like Mike and his brothers, but they also weren't suckers by any stretch of the imagination. The dad liked to hunt deer and string them up on his front porch.

Stack was in a car, shooting at Mike and his brothers. From their porch across the street I heard *BOOM! BOOM!* Mike's brothers must have had a .357 Magnum or something similar. The shots sounded louder than anything I had ever heard in my young life. *BOOM! BOOM! BOOM!* Then the car pulled off and the smoke cleared, and I mean that literally—I watched the gun smoke float up and away.

Here was the problem, though: Stack lived right down the street from Mike and them. Those guys shot at each other off and on for three days, right there on the block, all because of some argument. Police would come by, asking if anybody saw anything. We'd all say, "Nah, man, we ain't seen nothing," and then the police would leave. A couple hours later, more shots.

I had heard guns being used before, and had seen a couple guys bust them, watching from our window above the store. This time, though, I was almost in the middle of the action. Keith and I smelled the gunpowder. It was scary at first. But after a couple days of them shooting back and forth, most of the fear wore off and I began to take it for granted that every day I'd have to be ready to duck gunshots. And that feeling of routine is almost worse than the feeling of overwhelming fear. When violence becomes part of your daily existence, it changes you forever. I walk around today in Beverly Hills and whenever I hear a loud sound or see someone running, my fight-or-flight reflexes kick right in. I never want to be caught in that no-man's-land.

Here's another thing: Countries war with each other over deep beliefs, or commodities, or centuries of history. I was in the middle of a war over feelings, or the lack thereof. A war over bad communication. Edmonton Avenue was supposed to be a neighborhood, which should signify neighbors creating a community together. And we did have that, through the efforts of my father and other people who cared. But disrespect and violence sometimes tore neighbors apart, turning our neighborhood into a soulless hood.

. . .

Dad started giving me ten dollars every day for lunch money. When our report cards came in, he'd give Brandie, Meco, and me twenty dollars for every A, ten for a B, and five for a C. Most of my report cards were straight A's, so that's a hundred twenty, maybe a hundred forty dollars. I would take that windfall and use it to win even more money shooting dice.

See, sometimes you win not because of luck or skill, but because the size of your bankroll allows you to outlast your opponent. You know he can't keep hitting points forever. "You got to be able to stand the rain," my dad told me. "Sooner or later they got to crap out, and that's when you get your money." When I realized that money makes money, or at least makes it easier to make more money, I had yet another strategy for stacking. By the time I got to fifth grade at Chambers Elementary, I was taking three or four hundred dollars to school with me every day. I owned every pair of Jordans, and a pager. I started talking to different girls, including one cutie named Candace, and bought them a bracelet or a purse here and there. I also had a baby face and was small even for my young age; at ten or eleven I still looked eight. Older people couldn't compute how someone so young was doing what I was doing and dressed the way I did. That just added to the growing mystique of Little Rich.

I was ironing my clothes for school one morning when a thought came into my mind. I laid all my cash on the board and ironed the bills flat. A few of them turned brown from the heat, but that was OK. The way the ironed bills stacked and folded on each other just felt right to me.

. . .

I had a friend at Chambers Elementary named Thomas. As bad as things were for me at home, Thomas had it way worse. A lot of times the electricity at his house got turned off, sometimes the heat got turned off in the middle of an Ohio winter. He might come to school smelling like piss. On top of all that, Thomas had a big ol' bottom lip. Other kids ranked on him relentlessly, but I took a liking to him. Everyone's struggle is different—I'd learned that watching people come in and out of my father's store, everyone carrying their own special weight. I had a shield over my struggles, because my dad was around even when my mom wasn't. He'd also taught me how to make a little bit of money so I could stay in fresh gear, always cleaned and pressed. No matter how much things were unraveling at home with Mom, I never looked the part of a kid in crisis. But Thomas couldn't hide what he was going through.

In addition to giving me lunch money, a lot of days Dad brought me McDonald's or whatever else I wanted for lunch. On those days, he'd take me to school in the morning and ask what I wanted. I'd tell him a McDonald's Number 2 meal or whatever, and then he'd drop it off at school later, or pay a guy named Sam to drop it off for me. Sam moved to our neighborhood from North Carolina but had trouble finding work and maybe drank too much. My dad wanted to help him out, but not by just giving him money. My dad believed that just giving out money would hurt a man's pride and make him dependent instead of productive. So my dad paid Sam to bring my McDonald's to school, drop me off at basketball practice, or just stock coolers in the store. Sam is still in the neighborhood to this day, doing fine.

One morning Dad asked for my order and I told him a ten-piece McNuggets. Then for some reason I pulled a few bills from my pocket and said, "Make that two ten-pieces, please. I'm gonna buy one for my friend Thomas."

Dad gave me a long look and said, "That's how you do it, son."

My dad understood the 360-degree ecosystem of our neighborhood and the need to maintain some kind of balance in that world. He knew that his own success could help another person get ahead, whether that meant being in a position to give someone in need a part-time job or some credit until payday. Success could be shared. That didn't mean there weren't winners and losers—we had a lot of hard-core dice throwers who knew that their victories came out of somebody else's pocket. But things functioned best when winners won with class, losers maintained their dignity, and there was balance and fairness in the competition.

Dad could be a helping hand, but he gave you what you needed, not necessarily what you wanted. That's how our world functioned best. Sometimes that meant Dad giving out a few dollars, sometimes it was a job, sometimes it was tough love. When it came to his only son, Dad knew I needed to learn how to get what I needed to survive and thrive in the jungle. His way was to show me how to go get it myself, without hovering or constant intervention. "I can't live it for you," he always said. "What I can do is paint the picture."

. . .

Today, I try to have that same feel for the NBA ecosystem. I talk to our athletes about way more than basketball—finance, the best schools for their kids, whether to marry or move on from their girlfriends. At the same time, I'm not one of those agents who calls every day. Agents who call every day are walking on eggshells, not because they care so much, but because they're keeping an eye on their asset. Now, an athlete's ego can feed off that. But a well-fed ego is not, in the end, helpful to the athlete—vanity can ultimately destroy you. So my policy is: Don't feed the ego. The relationship I have with my guys is simple. You can call me anytime, I can call you anytime, and we can talk about whatever. But when you call me and it's a real situation, I will always give you what you need: the honest truth.

. . .

I don't remember Mom being high around us. If she was using, she just didn't come home, which meant I never saw her in the act of destroying herself—a blessing in disguise. Even though it hurt not to have her around, I love her for protecting us from seeing her smoking crack.

One day when we still lived above the store, Mom was out using when Dad came upstairs to check on us. He walked in and asked us where she was. Brandie said something a little smart like "Out doing what she shouldn't be doing." Brandie had it the hardest when it came to my mom, because in a lot of ways she had to be the mother for me and Meco. Brandie's resentment wouldn't let her love Peaches the way she really wanted to.

Dad told us all to sit down at the kitchen table. "Listen, your mom has a drug addiction, but she's still your mom. Don't ever let me catch you disrespecting her. It's a sickness, OK? You treat your mother with the respect she deserves. I don't want to have to ever have this conversation again."

When a man who doesn't repeat himself says that, you listen.

My father always took care of my mother, no matter what position she was in, no matter what his wife or anybody else said. He knew he could never be her true partner, and he wasn't *in* love with her, but he definitely loved her and cared about her well-being. The arrangement may have seemed odd to outsiders, but he was his own man, and if somebody didn't like it, so be it. Now, Dad loved hard, and at times I could see the hurt and disappointment he felt over what Mom was doing. Dad knew the type of smarts that Mom had and wanted to help her make something out of it. That's why he moved her in above the store. But he was up against an epidemic. Crack was taking over the neighborhood. No matter what interventions anyone might try, Mom was still surrounded by temptation and opportunity. Back then, you could buy crack easier and cheaper than a pack of cigarettes. As more and more people got hooked on it, it changed the whole dynamic of the block.

There were more robberies and break-ins, because fiends would do anything for that next hit. Gunshots between rival dealers and crews became more frequent. More kids ran around unsupervised, because their parents were high. Like my mom.

She wasn't a bad person, or stupid, or selfish. She loved the hell out of us kids. Like my father said, addiction is a disease that can strike anyone. Why do some people take a drink or a smoke and then stop, while other people get hooked? At least some of that is related to the body and brain chemistry we're born with. For whatever set of reasons—circumstances or hardwiring or bad judgment or some combination thereof—my mom was someone who could not resist drugs. That obviously took a toll on her relationship with my dad, because as much as you can try to help a drug user, as much as you think you can save them, addiction can be stronger than love.

It should be obvious by now that my dad was a player. Peaches wasn't his only girlfriend; far from it. The back stockroom to the store also had a couch in it. Once or twice my mom came by and another woman was back there. I never saw that, but my sister remembers Peaches wreaking havoc on those women, dragging them outside and beating them *down*. After she ran the women off, she went back inside and tore the store up. I told you, Peaches was a firecracker. When she went off, you better duck.

But most of the time Mom just wasn't there. One day she left us alone with Aunt San, who had Down's syndrome. I was about three years old, which would make Meco six and Brandie about eight. We were hungry, so Aunt San and Brandie decided to fry some fish. The hot oil was bubbling and Aunt San asked Brandie to go turn the fish over. Brandie was hardly big enough to see over the stove, and when she tried to turn the fish, the pan flipped and splashed boiling oil all over Brandie's face.

This was before cellphones, so we had no way to contact Mom. Brandie's face was blistering. She called Grandma Ruth's house and Uncle Ernest told her to put butter on the burns, but the oil was still hot so the butter was literally cooking on Brandie's face. They called an ambulance and took Brandie to the hospital. She had second- and third-degree burns on her face and neck, but when the doctors asked why her mother wasn't home and who was watching us, Brandie made up a story. Later we found out that when Brandie got burned, Mom was at the bar across the street.

Another time, one of our neighbors became concerned and called social services, and they sent a woman to our place to check on us. While the social services lady was knocking on the front door, Brandie jumped out the second-floor window, ran up the block to a grown-up friend's house, and brought the friend back to our house to pretend *she* was our mother. Brandie didn't want us to get separated in the foster care system.

It's hard to feel love for your mother when those types of things are happening.

In June of 1990, when I was nine and a half years old, Grandma Ruth moved back to St. Louis and decided to take me, Brandie, and Meco with her. She basically took custody of us away from her daughter. I don't know if Grandma was fed up with how we were being raised, or if Mom asked her to do it—maybe both. There might have been some discussion about Dad taking me in, but nobody wanted to split up me and my siblings in different cities. I don't know where Mom lived during this time, but it wasn't in St. Louis. The day we left is the only time I ever saw Dad with tears in his eyes. I remember that the Jordan 5s were just coming out, white with the reflective tongue, and I refused to leave Cleveland without getting those shoes. For some reason, at that moment when my whole life was being torn apart and I was being separated from both of my parents, I fixated on those shoes. Maybe I wanted some kind of consolation. Maybe I needed something solid and real to focus on, something of real worth, real beauty, real value, something that wouldn't let me down. The U-Haul truck was in the driveway, but I insisted that somebody take me to MC Sports to get those sneakers. Someone did. I came home with the shoes, got in the truck, and we drove to St. Louis.

My grandmother moved us into a big old house on Garfield and Natural Bridge Road. I was mad at everything about St. Louis. I was mad that Grandma Ruth made us clean up the big old yard. I was mad that one particular Auntie would visit and make us fold our clothes and put them away. She had escaped a lot of the pitfalls that my mother and the rest of the older siblings experienced, because she saw firsthand how destructive crack was in their lives and avoided it for herself. She had a good man in her life, a steady job in St. Louis as a welder, and lived in a well-kept brick house with a

Lincoln parked in the driveway. That was great for Auntie, but she had no empathy or understanding for my mom's situation. The older siblings took all the blows that helped show Auntie the right path, but Auntie criticized them. We got sent over to Auntie's house a lot when Grandma went to work, and she would tell me, Brandie, and Meco to go play in the basement. We heard her bad-mouthing my mother because her voice came through the vents. It made me angry and confused, but her words also began to turn me against my mother. This is the first time I can recall thinking, *Ain't no love.* Us three kids were being toted around like extra baggage. Dad mailed us food stamps and cash, but he was back in Cleveland. We had no idea where Mom was.

Auntie ended up getting hooked on dope herself. She lost her Lincoln, her man, and her house. She lost every single thing.

RULE

**Study Your Craft.**

## 7

# THE KID

A green money carpet is spread at my feet. A few more bills float down as I grip the dice in my eleven-year-old fist. I'm wearing the Jordan Grapes, standing behind a church on 105th Street in Cleveland, surrounded by grown men. Everybody is loud-talking and signifying, but I'm having my own private conversation.

"What's it gonna be?" I whisper to my two best friends. "We got this?"

The dice answered me back. They always did.

*No doubt*, the dice told me. *We good.*

Yes, the dice used to talk to me. I'm very serious when I say that. The more money at stake, the more involved our conversations became. Inside my head, I could literally hear their voice. On this particular day in 1991 the dice told me,

*You know how we do. Stop worrying and let us fly.*

After seven months in St. Louis I was back in Cleveland, living with my mom, Brandie, and Meco in an apartment my dad had in Euclid. My infatuation with dice remained in full effect. I studied the older gamblers, watching how they bet, their mannerisms, how they read the action. When my opportunity came, I was ready.

A hustler named Dave sold dope near the store. Dave's brother Willie Wild also sold some dope but was a professional gambler; he only sold the dope to get his gambling money. Willie Wild shot a lot of dice by the store, and I managed to edge into some of those games and make an impression on him. There's no age requirement in the hood. As long as you have money, you're in play. And I always had money.

Willie Wild was in his early twenties at the time, slim, charismatic, and dark-skinned, with a clean-shaven bald head that made him look like Michael Jordan if he shot dice instead of a basketball. He grew up in Mississippi, rolling dice in the dirt. Once he got to Cleveland, Willie always looked for a place to shoot that had some dirt on the ground, because he knew techniques for shooting the dice onto soft landing spots. This was when I started to understand that shooting dice was anything but pure luck. It was a skill, something that guys practiced. At least the guys who won. Willie Wild drove up to the corner by the store one day with his window down, and I asked where he was going.

"To take these niggas' money behind the church up 105th." The way he looked at me felt like a challenge.

"Can I come?"

Willie's passenger door swung open.

When we got to the game the men there at first didn't want to let me play, because they thought I was eight years old instead of eleven. But Willie vouched for me, and so did my roll of bills. A well-known OG named Wink finally said, "His money green. Let him play."

Right away I'm hot, betting fifty or a hundred on the fade, which means I'm betting on the shooter to lose. They roll seven, roll eleven, I'm winning. Now it's my turn to shoot and I roll a five. That's my "point"—I need to roll another five to win.

Before I shoot again, I make a nine-five side bet. See, in my mind I know every combination of what the dice look like on all sides when they land. I know that if I roll a four-and-one combination, then one side of each die—not facing up, but on one side— will possibly be a five or a four, which, if both appear, adds up to nine. The same thing applies if I roll a three and a two—there's a possibility that the sides of the dice will have a six-three combination, which adds up to nine. So my nine-five side bet means I'm extremely confident that not only will I roll a five, but I'll do it so that the sides of the dice *also* add up to nine. These are some of the combinations my dad taught me.

*Boom*—I jump the point. That means on my very next roll, I shoot the nine-five combination and win. When you jump a point you're not just winning, you're winning emphatically. It feels like a dunk in basketball. Now my point is six. I bet a straight six, which means no side bet. To win, all I have to shoot is a combination of one-five, two-four, or three-three. I roll a few times and avoid seven and eleven—if I hit those, I crap out and lose. Then I roll a six and win the point. Next I hit three tens in a row. That means I win three more rounds of betting by rolling a ten and then, without crapping out, roll another ten each time. Now I've hit five points in a row and the other guys are losing money. The odds are strongly against me winning a sixth point, so guys increase their bets to recoup their losses.

My next roll is a four. Four is one of the hardest points to hit in the game of craps. Now they know I'm gonna lose. The green carpet gets thicker. I held my friends close to my ear. They said the magic words:

*Stop worrying and let us fly.*

I jumped that four with a deuce-deuce and *man,* it was complete pandemonium. When all the noise died down, Wink spoke a line from the movie *Purple Rain* that the club owner said about Prince:

"The Kid is in rare form tonight."

From that day on, in dice games all around the city, I was known as the Kid.

. . .

Dad's apartment in the suburb of Euclid was what hustlers used to call a honeycomb hideout, an out-of-the-way place he could lie low and get into whatever he wanted to get into without his wife knowing. We lived in apartment 510 of the Americana, which had a view of Lake Erie and felt like a luxury building to us. It only had one bedroom, though, so I was back to sleeping on the floor. Dad's plan was for us to stay there until Mom could get better. Instead, she got worse. She was never home, so it ended up being me, Brandie, and Meco on our own.

I got myself up every morning and either took the city bus to Upson Elementary School, which had a lot of white students, or walked. I was in the fourth grade. I made friends with a white kid at Upson, Dennis, who lived down the street from our school, and sometimes we went by his house during lunch period. It was a normal single-family house, nothing lavish, with a side door that opened directly into the kitchen. That's when I realized that not all white people were wealthy.

Dad gave me and my siblings spending money and grocery money whenever we asked, but I didn't see him every day. I didn't go to the store in the mornings before school when I lived at the Americana, because it was about a fifteen-minute drive away. I didn't see him after school, either; at that time of day, Uncle Joe held down the counter while Dad was out handling his business. Dad had a lot going on, including a wife and daughter, and he didn't feel the need to check in with me daily and ask if I was OK. He felt like he had taught me well enough that I would come find him if I needed something.

I was only ten years old, and my maturity and discipline with money were still undeveloped. So even though Dad gave us money, some days, my pockets were empty. On those days, after school I had to hustle up some money to eat. I don't consider this as being neglected, but as being given a lesson in how to survive—how to "get it how you live." If I needed money, first I'd stop by the store and ask Uncle Joe for twenty dollars out of the cash register. I'd use that twenty to gamble on dice, tunk, or shooting jumpers. I had a nice jump shot from practicing on that crate at the Dust Bowl and won a lot of money shooting from the top of the key. I'd put the twenty dollars back in Dad's register, then take my winnings to the convenience store by our apartment and buy bread, sliced turkey breast, cheese, and milk. At first I bought gallons of juice, but we drank that so fast, I switched to Kool-Aid because it came in packets and we could stretch it. If push came to shove, I could make a grilled cheese sandwich, but plenty of nights all I had was bread and butter. Sometimes all I had was sugar water.

Other times my jump shot or the dice might not be falling right. There was a little bar by our apartment called the Grill, and they had amazing cheeseburgers with grilled bread that cost a dollar and ten cents. I'd walk around the parking lot of our building or comb the streets around the convenience store, finding a dime here and a nickel here, until it added up to enough for a cheeseburger. I had no idea where my mother was.

I was never into horseplay as a kid, or playing Nintendo or Atari, or running around in the street laughing and joking with my friends. I had to always be thinking about how I would make it to the next day. Even now, as an adult, I don't fool around just to be passing time. My mind is fixed on making the most of the moment. *Let's get to it.*

My only indulgence was sports. My dad paid for basic cable and I stayed up watching baseball and basketball games coming in from the West Coast. I liked to watch a whole game from beginning to end, including the interviews with the players afterward. The games came on at ten and didn't go off until one in the morning. My favorite player was Rickey Henderson, number 24 with the Oakland A's. As always, I didn't just watch the game, but took in the whole culture around the game, the players, the strategies, the style, and the aesthetics. I noted how the big green letters spelling ATHLETICS across the front of Rickey's jersey popped against the white background. I focused on the things I could study and master so I wouldn't get lost in a world that was spinning out of control. I stayed up late watching those games, eating grilled cheese or butter sandwiches, studying statistics and the words of the athletes and analysts, then got up the next morning and went to school. That was my life.

RULE

**Move with Intention;
Be Ready to Improvise.**

# 8

# A CERTAIN WAY

Dad's lease at the Americana ended and we had to move again. Toward the end of 1991, I moved in with Dad's mom, Grandma Johnnie Mae Paul, at her house on 11610 Scottwood Avenue, between 123rd and Lakeview. Brandie and Meco moved in with our Uncle Kevin on 141st and Shaw in East Cleveland—our first time living apart. It was a twenty-minute walk from Granny's house on Scottwood to R&J Confectionary, where I was once again spending most of my time.

Grandma Johnnie Mae's house was a nice single-family, two-story home. For the first time in my life I had my own bedroom, even though it was barely twice as wide as my twin bed. Johnnie Mae was an orderly woman, fair-skinned to the point of looking almost white, with long hair. Her husband had died a few years earlier. She worked at University Hospital as some sort of supervisor, and had a strict regimen like I'd never seen. She got up at three-thirty every morning and went to bed at five-thirty each night while watching *Golden Girls, Columbo,* and *Murder, She Wrote* on the TV on top of her bedroom dresser. I liked to sit on the floor in her room, wait until she fell asleep, then change the channel to sports. Once I found what I wanted, maybe the Bulls game on WGN, I had to keep the sound down so she wouldn't wake up. Living with her meant I had to slow myself down to her pace, be quiet and patient, a different speed than the fast life on the block. Johnnie Mae was very detail-oriented, she wanted things done the right way the first, second, and third time. Every morning, she cooked me two sausage links with either French toast or a boiled egg. I had stopped drinking coffee because I heard it would stunt my growth and I wanted to be an NBA player, so she made me tea. She washed my clothes for me every day and ironed everything, including my underwear. I saw her feed and bathe her own mother, my great-grandmother, with the same kind of love and dedication. Johnnie Mae Paul lived her life with precision and intention, the way poor Black people have always done to keep things together when there's chaos outside the door. She gave me chores, like cutting the grass or the hedges, and when I was done she wrote me checks for ten dollars, which I cashed at Dad's store. I never got checks from anybody else. Every year on my birthday, Grandma Johnnie Mae made me a three-layer German chocolate cake. Every single year. Like I said: precision, consistency, and intention.

My Uncle Charlie lived with us, and he applied the same rigor to his life. Uncle Charlie had served in the military and still operated on a soldier's strict schedule. He watched *Larry King* and *Meet the Press* religiously. He went to sleep at ten P.M. on the dot every night, wearing a stocking cap on his head. He woke up at six every morning. Every Tuesday morning at ten sharp he left the house to see his girlfriend, wearing dress shoes, a crisp white dress shirt, jeans, and a Borsalino hat. He drove a sky blue four-door Ford Tempo that was clean enough to eat off. He returned every Wednesday at eleven in the morning, with the exact amount of groceries in the trunk to last one week.

This is one of the ways that Black people have survived in America. When the dangers unleashed by the system threaten to spin through our lives like a tornado, we do things a certain way—consciously, purposefully—to avoid being swept away. Ain't no stumbling your way through life. Black folks don't have enough margin of error for that. Most of us have no margin of error at all.

But even with all that discipline, you still never know what might happen—you have to plan with intent but always be ready to improvise.

. . .

Remember those five wild brothers who lived on Edmonton—Mike, Slim Black, Onnie, Deron, and Tommy? We called them "pistoleros," because they were experts at handling their firearms.

They came up in the '70s, when handguns usually carried only six bullets, so they had to make each bullet count. Plus, they had to cock back the hammer before each shot because those guns didn't fire thirty times and spray all over the place like a semiautomatic. Nah. You had to aim.

One Christmas morning, Onnie got in an argument with his father, and his father shot Onnie dead, right there in the family living room, within sight of Dad's store. Merry Christmas.

With Onnie gone, the most dangerous brother was understood to be Slim Black. He wasn't the only known killer on the block. There was Ernie from the Eddy Road side of Edmonton who had a serious reputation. We had Shady G, an older dude who stuttered when he robbed guys: "Y-y-y-y-you know what it is." I watched the body of his baby's mother, Patricia, deteriorate over time from shooting so much dope into her veins. Shady G's son is doing seventeen years in prison now. B Rob was another killer; he worked as a hit man for a hustler named Fat G, who weighed about three hundred and fifty pounds. Fat G sponsored a youth league football team, and sometimes he sat in his car during games with a pile of crack rocks and a shotgun and sold dope out the window. Fat G gained even more weight over the years, about doubled in size, and when he died they had to cut open his house around the door to get his body out.

But among the ranks of Glenville killers, Slim Black was near the top. We all interacted on a regular basis with people we knew had committed murder—but it wasn't a big deal. Your neighbors are your neighbors. I was mindful of who Slim Black was, but I didn't fear or avoid him because, well, he lived up the block. Wasn't no avoiding him even if we wanted to. More importantly, Dad had known all the brothers since they were pups. At some point they might have even done some muscle-type work for Dad; he liked to keep a few of those types around. I think that's why Dad gave Mike a pistol that day I got caught in the shootout. But when my dad went legit, with no more monkeypaw or after-hours joint, he didn't need them for muscle anymore.

And then Slim Black and some of his brothers started smoking crack, which made them even more dangerous than before.

One day I was working in the store when Slim Black walks in. He was a handsome guy, tall and dark-skinned. He always wore his baseball cap cocked on his head ace-deuce, balanced almost like a book. Even when he wore a skullcap in the winter, he rolled it up ace-deuce to the side. Slim Black was wearing a leather jacket with his hands in his pockets. Wasn't no telling what else he had in those pockets, a knife, a gun, a stick of dynamite. You didn't play around with Slim Black.

He walked to the cooler and came to the counter with a $1.99 bottle of Olde English malt liquor.

"Ay Big Rich, lemme get this forty of Old Gold and I'll bring you back the money."

I kept the same expression on my face, but inside my Spidey-senses went up. Slim Black had been through the store a few weeks ago and took another forty on credit, and still hadn't paid for that one. Now here he was, freeloading again. What was Dad gonna do?

Dad paused for a few seconds, then said, "Go 'head, you got it."

Slim Black started to slide out; Dad interrupted his exit.

"Yo Slim, you know you owe me that other money, right?"

Slim Black turned back around. "I got you, Big Rich. I'm gonna take care of you."

"Alright then, because you know you ain't getting nothing else 'til you pay me my money."

That was a master class for me in people management and conflict resolution, one of many examples of Dad dealing with the most dangerous and unpredictable people in a way that kept things running smoothly. Sometimes in the neighborhood you had to fight fire with fire, meet aggression with aggression. But not always. Survival required constant calibrating and balancing various and sometimes competing factors. *Who is this person? What's the foundation of our relationship? What are they capable of? How much is at stake? What point is this person at in his or her life?* You had to consider all those variables, slow down, and move consciously.

. . .

I encounter so many situations in my business today where I use what I learned from watching my dad. It could be sitting in my office, negotiating with a guy who used to lead the deadliest gang in

Los Angeles, but who's now trying to make moves in sports and entertainment. But it could also be in a Hollywood boardroom, where I have to make it clear that I'm not intimidated by any of the power players around the table. The business world is full of dangerous people, not in terms of physical safety, but the kind of people who'll take everything from you and then go home and sleep like a baby. Even if your mind is moving a million miles an hour trying to figure out the right play, you never blink. The best strategy is always more than one step, one action. My dad let Slim Black get that forty—but that was only step one. Step two was to clarify for Slim Black that this forty would be the last. He avoided a dangerous confrontation with his first move, but the second move was the one that mattered: He made sure Slim Black left the store crystal-clear about the nature of their relationship and who was in control. Slim Black was killed a few years later. A guy took the No. 3 bus to our block, got off, and shot him dead in the street over some dispute. His son Little Slim just got killed last year, shot in the head. So much of our suffering is just a tragic repetition of what happened to our parents and their parents before them, the unbroken generational cycles that haunt us. It takes an exceptional person to break that cycle for himself and his family. My father was that person.

RULE

**Understand the Whole Show.**

## 9

# IF NOT FOR CRACK

In the 1960s and '70s, Cleveland had some of the best public schools in the country—but only if you were white. Black students were segregated into schools with less funding, broken-down buildings, outdated textbooks, and every other disadvantage you could think of. The NAACP filed a lawsuit against the city, and finally a judge determined that the state of Ohio and the Cleveland school district had intentionally created and maintained a system that separated Black students from white ones. Then the court ordered the city to do something about it. In 1979, about one year before I was born, the city started busing kids across town to achieve more racial balance in public schools.

This history smacked me in the face when I was twelve years old and starting the seventh grade. Instead of attending Patrick

Henry Middle School on the East Side, I got bused to Thomas Jefferson on the West Side. This was supposed to balance things out—bringing Black students to a predominantly white neighborhood and some of the white kids to our side of town. When the fall arrived, I was actually excited about it. I looked forward to attending school in a completely different environment. Then I got to Thomas Jefferson.

It turned out it was just as bad over there as on the East Side. Thomas Jefferson had white and Hispanic people, but we were all poor. We didn't even have gym class, because the school didn't have a gym. The ceiling was coming down, the floors were torn up, it was crazy. When the weather got nice, they put a rollaway hoop in the parking lot for us to play basketball on.

Like I said before, all you could see from Cleveland was more Cleveland.

Fortunately, I didn't have to rely on school for athletics. My neighborhood, Glenville, had extensive youth sports organizations, from elementary school on up, all run by local people in the community. We played a lot of baseball; there were multiple diamonds on a big open field near 114th Street and St. Clair. The league was run by the Glenville Youth Athletic Association, with games six days of the week. Us kids had all the equipment we needed, nice gloves and bats that we carried around in our baseball bags. The games were packed, everybody's family and friends watching, burgers and sodas and ice cream for sale. When the bigger kids played a night game, it could turn into a major event. I was always small for my age, but became known in my neighborhood for being good at sports. My dad didn't come that often to any of my games in various sports; he was busy running the store and doing the things he had to do. The man did have another family, after all. When he did show up, he relaxed in a lawn chair with a cooler and a fifth of Burnett's gin, accompanied by a lady who my friends laughed about being "somebody's mama." My own mother never came to my games, not that I expected her to or even hoped she would. I felt good about myself regardless, wearing fresh batting gloves, wristbands, and cleats that I bought with my dice winnings. For one game, I showed up in the Deion Sanders Diamond Turf sneakers. Wearing the hottest shoes out for a *baseball* game, where they were bound to get dirty? That was insane. We also played pickup baseball games on our own, with full teams of nine guys each. It seems strange now to think about baseball being such a big deal in the hood, and if you go by 114th and St. Clair now, all those baseball fields are just weeds. There are very few African Americans in Major League Baseball now. But in the early 1990s baseball was still extremely popular in the Black community, so during the summertime it was our number one sport.

I liked baseball but showed the most talent in football. Ohio is a football state, with some of the best high school teams in the country. Cleveland is a football city, with the long history of the Browns, so we all grew up loving the game. We started out playing in the street and, at about age ten, progressed to the organized "municipal" games known as Muny League. Games were at Bump

Taylor Field, which was right in the middle of all the action, across Eddy Road from the rough end of Edmonton. This league was highly organized, with good coaching and strict weight limits for each division. On weigh-in days, some of the heavier kids stood on the scale wearing nothing but a jockstrap, butt cheeks all out, trying to get under the maximum weight. A couple times our dominant nose tackle, Chocolate, was too heavy, and coaches made him wear a trash bag and run laps to sweat the weight off. It was that serious. The stands were full for every game. Even though we took it pretty seriously, there wasn't the huge amount of pressure on young players like there is now, so a lot of parents just took it as a chance to socialize and hang out among themselves, eating Raider Dogs and just kicking it. Sometimes I wish there had been more pressure on the players to become the best they could be. A lot of them had major talent but got drawn into the streets.

Kyle Bland was the best player of my generation in Cleveland, and to this day is the coldest football player I've ever seen in my life. Unbelievable speed, strong and quick, he had the whole package. There wasn't a punt that he didn't run back for a touchdown. One season Kyle scored twenty-eight touchdowns in eight games—and by the way, his shoulder pads were off by halftime because his team was blowing the opposition out. Kyle came from a good family, both of his parents worked, he had good grandparents over on Woodside, but in our neighborhood, once Muny League was over, you were off the porch and getting into the mix on the block. That's where Kyle ended up.

I played every position a small, fast kid could play: cornerback, receiver, safety, running back. I ended up starting at quarterback in Muny League, not because I was the best player, but because I could get the other kids to follow me. One of the wildest boys on our team was Kamal. He had serious anger issues. At practice he'd fly off the handle, cuss coaches out, grab a teammate by the face mask and sling him around. When Kamal was all the way out of pocket, I'd talk to him calmly and he'd simmer down. "It ain't that serious, man, we good. Next play," I'd tell him. Or, "Let's just finish up practice and then go down to the store, I'll treat you to whatever you want." Kamal listened to me.

Candace, my friend from Chambers Elementary, was a cheerleader at Muny League, and we started dating. I enjoyed the feeling of being the star quarterback with the prettiest girl. Candace's mother had drug problems, like mine. When I think now about how pervasive addiction was in our community, it feels crazy. It *was* crazy. But at that time, it felt completely normal. Crack was all around us, all day every day, being bought, sold, smoked, chased, even killed over. It affected every aspect of life in Glenville. But to us, it was just another day in the neighborhood.

Another friend whose mom was on dope was Carlos. Carlos and I had been tight from about first grade. We played football together, and he lived not far away, on Ohlman Avenue, with his grandmother and his brother. Carlos was a good player, but by the time he was twelve years old he was off the porch and didn't care so much about football. He started smoking weed early, selling dope early, carrying the pistol and taking no shit early. His brother, Big Head Boo, had a lock on his bedroom door, a waterbed in his room, a refrigerator, girls sleeping over. When I was still in middle school, sometimes I spent the night there and slept on the floor. We'd stay up late washing our helmets or spatting our cleats. Saturday mornings we walked down to the football field for our game. Big Head Boo sold dope right out of his second-floor crib and was open all night. When he was too tired to walk downstairs, he'd throw a pill bottle downstairs, the customer put the money in a bottle and tossed it up, and then Boo dropped the drugs back down in the bottle. Carlos followed in his brother's footsteps and became known as "2 Los." He'd go from playing football to playing the streets and balling at the mall. When Carlos was maybe eleven years old, he accidentally shot himself in the calf waiting for the school bus. He had to wait for the wound to heal before he could get back on the field.

Heartbreaking, right?

Not to us. We knew dozens of Carloses in Glenville. There were more all across Cleveland, and in Black communities across America. That's why I say, if you didn't live through the crack era, it's hard to fully understand just how much it defined our lives. It was hard for us to know at the time. It was just life.

One of my best friends was a kid named Holyfield. His actual name was Damon, but everybody called him Holyfield because he looks just like the heavyweight champion boxer, and he was known for fighting dudes and putting them to sleep. One day I walked over to Holy's house on 123rd to pick him up for football practice. Holy had my bike at his house, plus I needed to check up on him. We had to get permission slips signed and pay fifteen dollars for the season fee. He was my tailback and I needed to make sure all his paperwork was straight. That was my job as the leader.

I knocked on Holy's door and an adult I didn't know let me in. When I walked into the living room, the first thing I saw was crack rocks piled high on a plate. Like, a mountain of rocks. Holy's dad sold dope. The spot was jumping, fiends coming in and out. I swear there had to be about two thousand rocks on the plate.

Holy came out of his room and his father said, "Y'all get on up outta here." As kids we knew to stay out of grown folks' business, because if we didn't they were quick to bring out a belt or punch you in your chest. We stayed out of it, but we also knew what was really going on. Still, this might have been the first time I saw that amount of crack and this many fiends all in one small indoor space. I was sort of shook and had to get my bearings. I'm about eleven years old, trying to make sure my friend has his permission slip and his fifteen bucks to play football, but first I got to navigate this hellscape. For Holy, it was home. It was where he laid his head every night. We managed to get the permission slip signed, then I sat on the handlebars of my bike while Holy rode us to practice.

Holy is another one of those kids who could have benefitted from more emphasis on sports. When he started hustling, and got into all the things that go along with that lifestyle, his performance on the field suffered. Holy could have been a Division 1 tailback or cornerback, if not for crack.

One football season I was determined to win the Lee Memorial Trophy. From the time practice started in July, I was super focused on taking it home. The trophy went to the most important player on the team based on leadership, playing ability, the whole package. That was 50 percent of my fixation on it. The other half was that the trophy resembled the actual Heisman Trophy, the award given to the best player in college football. I could envision it on the mantel at my grandma's house.

First, I figured out who the voters were. I discovered that I knew several adults who not only voted, but were influential in the entire award process. I made sure that I showed them all my report cards, which were A's and a few B's. I arrived first at the field for every practice, led the warm-up exercises, and finished first in every conditioning lap. Our team was really good that year, too. I left nothing to chance, and sure enough, when the banquet came, I won the Lee Memorial Trophy. Holyfield won MVP.

Walking up to the stage to accept the trophy I had dreamed about was an emotional moment. From having watched all those player interviews on TV, I knew the athletes always thanked people after a win or accolade, so when I walked up on stage to get my award, I started off with "I'd like to thank the cheerleaders . . ." Holyfield still laughs about that. (If we're keeping it real, I did date more than a few of them.)

It was one of the highest points of my life up to then. Neither of my parents was there.

. . .

Football was my first love, but when I started playing basketball, it felt a little bit more sexy. I could get fly on the basketball court, in terms of the accessories and the style of everything. We played most of our organized basketball at the Glenville Rec Center, where Vince Brookins, the director, genuinely cared for us kids. We called him Mr. Vincent. As a shooter I played the two. A kid named Amo was our point guard, and he was cold. I wished I could play like Amo. Kamal played the three, he was raw with it and had a great jump shot. Kamal and Amo were the nicest on our squad. Aaron Nichols was one of the best athletes in our neighborhood, his nickname was Showtime, or Show for short. He was younger than us but big for his age, and played a smart, cerebral game. My cousin Jason Betts was at the five. Off the bench we had Holyfield and one of my childhood friends from Eddy Road, Pill Mil.

Kamal is locked up now for killing his baby's mother's mother. My cousin Jason is fighting a murder charge; his first trial ended with a hung jury. He grew up with both parents, who had good jobs. When I used to go to Jason's house, I felt a calmness. He had an entertainment room where we watched TV. There was a picture on the wall of his grandmother's farm in Tennessee. I always looked at that picture and thought to myself, *Damn, they got something in their family they can appreciate.* Jason grew up comfortably, but our environment sucked him under. The first time he ever got arrested was for that killing. Show, our power forward, works with me now at Klutch.

The basketball uniforms in that era were T-shirts, not jerseys like today. We had red tees with GLENVILLE on the front and a number ironed on the back. They didn't give you shorts back then. Another reason basketball felt more fly than other sports was because you could come to the game in street clothes and then put on your uniform at the game. Our team dressed up like we were stars going to an NBA game, in all our best Tommy Hilfiger and Polo. We got a lot of girls' phone numbers when we played away games.

Early in my sixth-grade basketball season, a team from Fairfax blew us out by about forty points. We got better and won a bunch of games in a row. Toward the end of the season Mr. Vincent, who played college basketball at Iowa, took us to see an Ohio State vs. Iowa game. Our crew was walking through different shops at the arena and saw these dope gray Ohio State shorts with red script lettering that went with our Glenville T-shirts. We put all our money together, Mr. Vincent covered the rest, and we all got fresh.

One game, I arranged for the whole team to wear red Chuck Taylor sneakers to match our uniforms. The championship game happened to align with the new Jordan 8s dropping, in black and white versions. I copped both and brought them to the game. When we got to the gym I let my homie Pill Mil rock the black pair, even though they were too small for him. He was the only guy on the team who hadn't bought the 8s, and I wanted the whole squad to shine.

The championship game was broadcast on local cable access television, which was a big deal. Our opponent was Fairfax, the team that had blasted us earlier that year. I think they took us for granted, because we came out hot and had a lead at halftime. My three-pointer was hitting like crazy, the bleachers were packed, people yelling my name—I got so excited I was waving my arms after made baskets, galloping and pointing to the crowd.

When we were in the locker room at halftime, Mil was saying my shoes were too small for him and hurt his feet. That gave me an idea. When I took the floor to start the second half, I was no longer wearing white Js—I had the black ones on. You have to understand how coveted Jordans were at that time; just having one pair was a big deal. Coming out for the second half in a different-color pair? That was unprecedented. People started pointing at my feet and I heard my name buzzing around the gym. It felt great, and so did my three-ball. I finished the game with twenty points, was named MVP, and got interviewed on TV after the game.

The week that followed that game was the first time I felt like an actual celebrity. But I learned something else. The game is about skill and talent, but it's also still entertainment. Showmanship counts. I got just as much attention for the sneaker switch as for dropping twenty points.

RULE

**Focus Is Everything.**

## 10

# BEAR DOWN ON A FOUR

All through middle school, I went months without seeing my mom. Sometimes she came through the store, or I randomly saw her on the street. My older brother, Meco, had been selling drugs for a while now, and she'd pull up on him and his crew and hit them up for cash—*twenty from you, forty from you, boy I know you got sixty.* She didn't do this in a begging dope fiend way, but in an "I known you since you was in diapers, and I know you got a pocket full of money" type of way. She maintained her dignity but she got her money, too. If you bought a ten-dollar fish dinner off her and only had a twenty, there wouldn't be any change. Meco swears she sold food just to lighten the impact of putting the bite down on guys, to make them feel better about giving her their money. She stayed selling our clothes, too. Sometimes guys gave her twenty dollars just to retrieve the Billionaire Boys Club shirt or whatever clothes of ours she had hanging over the fence in front of wherever she was staying. Peaches's hustle game was strong.

Occasionally she pulled up on a block where I was hanging out and asked one of my friends, "You seen Richard?" Somebody would run and find me, and as soon as they told me my mom was looking for me, I knew Peaches was about to ask me for some money. I was fine with that. I loved her, and I knew that even if she was coming for money, she also genuinely missed me. Whatever I had, I shared. But I also had to keep my feelings in check. I never knew what would happen with her next.

Once I made a rare visit to see her at a little place she was staying in off Euclid, behind Stanton. When I walked in, I got to see how she'd been living all this time we were apart. She didn't have any furniture, just a hot plate, a couple chairs, and some blankets on the floor. I had stopped by the Mr. Hero shop on the way over and brought her a Romanburger, her favorite. We sat there on the floor together while she ate. I wanted to do something for her. I went to the corner store and brought her back a Pepsi, a bunch of her favorite candy bars, and some Newport cigarettes, her brand. I had lost money that day gambling and only had forty dollars on me, but I gave her all of it. I felt numb about everything, not angry or frustrated. I was glad she had a place to stay. My biggest fear was her having to live outside, so if she had a roof over her head, I was straight. I didn't pay attention to the holes in the walls or the roaches crawling on the floors. I didn't care about anything but my mom.

When it was time to leave, the numbness faded for a moment and I felt an overwhelming surge of sadness. I didn't know when I was going to see her again.

I realized years later that experiences like these with my mother also offered lessons, not all of them good. It honed my natural sensitivity. Today, I can quickly sense what my athletes need most, how to take care of them, and how to make them *feel* taken care of—without worrying too much about my own needs, at least in that moment when I'm trying to be attentive to *their* needs. Being a good agent isn't about false flattery and insincere attention, but it's also not about treating athletes in purely a transactional way. People know you genuinely care about them when you understand what they really need and act on it. Just like in that moment at my mom's place, I knew what would make my mother feel cared for, and my desire to give it to her was genuine.

Throughout my mom's struggles, I held on to memories of the caring, dynamic, principled woman I knew her to be. Once when I was little, she came into the room where Meco and I shared a bed and said, "Bring me your clothes that don't fit, I'm giving them to the Berrys down the street." And we knew that if we saw one of the Berry kids wearing our clothes on the block, we better not say a word about it. Mom would tear our ass up for that. Let Peaches see us teasing some other kid for not having a toy like ours—she'd snatch it from us, hand it to the other kid and say, "Now that's yours." Our parents valued the rules and habits that helped the whole community survive in the ghetto with a measure of dignity. The truth was the same for all of us: We could either succumb to the environment and sink into kill-or-be-killed mode, or we could devise a code that allowed us to hold on to our humanity, and our neighbors', too. My parents chose the latter. Not everyone did.

All of this instilled a set of principles in us about how people should be treated and how things should be done. As we got older and more involved in the streets, we carried those ideas with us. We knew we couldn't do something shady and then expect our crew to back us up. You could get exiled for stuff like that. We had to stand on our name and have integrity. If someone else proposed breaking the code, there was a good chance we'd call them out. I heard Meco tell guys, "Nah, man, you dead motherfucking wrong. Ain't nobody rolling with you on that." The same thing applied to making promises that you knew wouldn't be kept. We would never soup up a situation with no intention of following through, and then have somebody making moves and plans based on some fraudulent things we said.

That's another thing that's stuck with me in my life in business: Your word is supremely important, especially when people are staking their lives on it. It's part of the deeper code of the streets—without integrity, even when you're out hustling, you got nothing. And when you're caught out there lying or trying to bamboozle people, you can pay a steep price. A lot of people I encounter in business come from environments where you can do people dirty and not suffer any truly lasting consequences. But where I come from, that type of behavior can cost you everything.

There was a flip side to the positive lessons I got, intentionally and unintentionally, from my mother. Like I said, I learned from both my parents that love can be expressed in deeper ways than just words and gestures—true love is when you really *see* someone, pay attention, understand their genuine needs, and act on them. But in my relationships with women, I express love in a totally different way than people are used to, and it can come across as cold or unfeeling.

Years later, after I moved to Los Angeles, a woman I was seriously dating asked me about my brother. She wanted to know who he was seeing and how they met and where I hung out with them and all kinds of other things.

"Why are you asking so many questions?" I said in a tone that meant I wasn't going to answer them.

"Rich," she replied, "if I don't ask questions, how are we supposed to get to know each other?"

That slapped me in the face. She was asking simple questions and I immediately went cold. It was a revelation. *I've been living the wrong way this whole time.*

I still had some of the streets within me. As many valuable lessons as I learned growing up, I also had scars that might never fade away.

. . .

The same realizations have come to me in my life as a parent. I have a daughter who's in college, a son in high school, and a younger son. With my daughter, especially, I've had to understand the difference between the way she's come up and the way I did. Growing up hard like I did provided me with some essential tools for life—like how to be vigilant and aware in dangerous situations. But my daughter never had to walk down the street clutching her purse or holding her pepper spray in case some guy jumps out of the alley, the way my sister did. The way my daughter's been raised makes her more trusting of the world around her, which makes her vulnerable, maybe, to certain dangers. But I also envy her ability to approach the world without constant suspicion and hyper-awareness. Not just of physical danger, but of the kind of emotional danger my mother sometimes represented in my life. I protected myself from that kind of danger by putting up a wall around my feelings. It's hard to bring that wall down, even now, even with the people I care about the most. I see my daughter's relative vulnerability and I want to protect it.

Where I come from, vulnerability wasn't conducive to survival. It was bred out of us by our environment. It's a quality I'm still trying to learn as an adult, because it was never even a possibility when I was growing up. My mom never held my hand while walking me to school. I never had experiences with my mom like just watching cartoons together on a Saturday morning, or doing homework at the kitchen table, or just talking about my feelings. I had to stay hard, even around her. I could never just get comfy. I had to keep moving on.

The place I moved on to was the streets. And if I wasn't focused there, it would cost me. I had to be on my toes.

. . .

My friend Shorty Feets was a Jehovah's Witness who loved to shoot dice. We'd meet up at seven forty-five in the morning to map out all the dice games on different blocks that we planned to hit. This was about the seventh grade. When we gambled, we always bet with each other and we never bet on each other to lose. Shorty Feets's pet point was eight. When he shot the dice he liked to spell out "E-I-G-H-T!" really fast. That was his style. We would actually get upset if we missed an eight or a six on the dice. Those were the easiest points in our minds.

How could I not be confident? I felt like the dice and I had a real relationship. I had this thing where I would just bear down on a four—one of the hardest points to hit. "Bearing down" means maintaining extreme focus, locking in, doing everything with precision. No making jokes or throwing the dice behind my back. In basketball, if you make a couple threes in a row, then get two or three more buckets, you bear down by going strong to the hoop the very next time you touch the ball; don't toss up a heat-check stepback from twenty-five feet. I was so brash shooting dice, just winning a straight four wasn't enough for me. Neither was betting the ten-four combination, which meant I'd shoot a four with a ten on the side. No, I'm *also* betting that I'll roll the four deuce-deuce. That's how much confidence I had, and how much I would bear down. But there was strategy to it, because there's only two ways to shoot a four, so I have a 50 percent chance of shooting it deuce-deuce. That was me running odds in my head and knowing the game. All of this calculation is happening with grown men pressing me, talking loud or whispering in my ear, saying things to break my concentration or delivering some subtle threat to throw me off my game. My guys and I still consistently won money. We were kids in middle school who gambled with grown men, some of them dope dealers or worse, some of them carrying guns—and we took their money while they tried to knock us off our game.

That's where I learned how to handle pressure.

Noise is everywhere. I came into the NBA knowing that the chatter don't matter—only the results. Today, a lot of the chatter is comments on social media. There's a whole lot of batter in the chatter that has no value other than to fluff things up. Then there's the noise from rivals in my industry—negative text messages they send to my clients, anonymous leaks to the media, all delivered without the fear of any serious consequences. I learned long ago how to block that out. It's all about bearing down. That's why I never celebrate a deal. I don't crack open champagne when we sign contracts. You won't know whether I'm happy or sad. I'm bearing down on whatever is next.

RULE

**Never Submit to
Your Surroundings.**

## 11

## NO AGE LIMIT

We sold tons of E-Z Widers at my dad's store, the cigarette paper that folks rolled their weed in. We also sold Chore Boys, which people used to smoke crack. A Chore Boy was a brand of scouring pad that fiends used as a filter in their pipes. We cut up the pad into little squares, wrapped them individually in paper, and kept them under the counter. A customer would come in, buy a pack of cigarettes and a pint of Wild Irish Rose wine and say, "Lemme get a Chore." A box had three pads in it; we cut them up into fifty or sixty pieces and sold each one for a quarter. Then they'd leave the store and do what they do. Everywhere I went, I saw drugs being sold. Each block had a crew hustling crack, sometimes several crews. I couldn't even count the number of my friends and uncles who were selling.

I was about eleven years old when I decided it was time for me to get into the game. But not with crack.

My affinity for clothes and sneakers had grown. Gambling was good money, but sometimes I lost. To get what I wanted, I needed a more consistent hustle. Crack was too risky, too violent. And I didn't want to make money with the drug that was dragging my mother under. Plus, everybody on the block was selling crack because the money came so fast. Weed, on the other hand, was an underserved market. My dad sold monkeypaw when he was younger, and I thought that if he found out I was selling weed he might be mad at me, but not like he would if he found out I was moving coke. Also, weed was the drug dealers' drug. All the dope boys smoked weed, and they never ran out of money. Less competition, less risk, a higher-income customer base, and less chance of getting my ass whooped by my dad? Marijuana checked all the boxes.

I didn't even have to go out of my way to get into the game. One of my mom's brothers was heavy in the streets. I walked over to Unc's house and told him I needed some weed to sell.

"You serious?" Unc exclaimed.

"Yeah I'm serious. I need to make money."

"You already notorious with them dice though," Unc said. "Everybody talking 'bout the Kid taking grown folks' money, the Kid got this and the Kid got that."

"Yeah, but I need another source of income. I'm not gonna

hustle full-time, just to make some extra cash. I'm not dropping out of school or nothing. I like school. This is a side thing."

Unc knew all about my mom's drug problems. He knew I was on my own a lot of the time and needed to be able to take care of myself. He grabbed his car keys and we drove to his stash spot. There were a couple bales of weed there, almost the size of the hay bales you see on a farm. One of his guys was bagging it up, surrounded by hundreds of ounce-sacks of weed. Unc gave me an ounce, plus a stack of small baggies for when I broke the ounce down.

"OK, look, if this is what you wanna do, here's how you do it," Unc said. "Be careful. Don't keep the product on you. Watch the people who are watching you. Be reliable, that's how you build loyal customers. And one more thing: This right here is primo herb. Ain't no better on the whole East Side. Price it accordingly."

I hit the scene selling twenty-dollar sacks, while most every-thing else went for five or ten. My price point was firm. I wouldn't take fifteen dollars, not seventeen, not eighteen. No three-for-fifty, no IOUs. I told everybody, "You have to pay for the best," and they respected that. Once the quality of the product became known, my pager started blowing up. As my hustle increased, some of my friends tried to get me to sell cocaine with them. From a competi-tive standpoint I was interested, because I always wanted to com-pete at the highest level. But I always said no because of the risk—both of getting caught and of my father's disapproval. And it still didn't sit right with me to sell the drug that was destroying my mother. I stuck to weed. After school I'd drop my book bag at the store, then hit the block for a couple hours to sell some weed and shoot some dice. I'd go practice whatever sport was in season, grab my book bag before the store closed at seven-thirty. Get home to Scottwood before Grandma Johnnie Mae and Uncle Charlie closed everything down for the night. Do my homework, watch some TV. That was my middle school routine.

My uncle underestimated how soon I'd come back for a re-up. The money piled up quickly. So did my purchases. I started keeping my clothes and sneakers in a little room in the basement of Grandma's house. I got a phone line that only rang down there. I didn't bring any girls to the little room, not yet, although I talked to a whole lot of them on my new phone. My wardrobe took a step up, of course. Anything Hilfiger or Polo, I had it, in every color. I bought a fat gold herringbone necklace that drew double takes from my friends.

What really set me apart, though, was the bike.

In the seventh grade, I spent two thousand dollars to customize my bicycle. I started with a Dyno that I bought from the store for four hundred. I took it to the paint shop and had them strip it all the way down to the metal, then redo it in purple. I bought gold 144-spoke Dayton rims, a crushed velvet banana seat, new handlebars, custom grips. This was the most expensive bike anybody on the East Side had ever seen, being pedaled by a twelve-year-old kid.

I was still at my father's store every day, working the register if they needed me but also just hanging out. Now I could gamble with Uncle Joe; we'd stand up a milk crate behind the counter and play tunk. A couple guys would come through and we'd shoot dice in the back for three, four hundred dollars a roll.

I bought my first pistol about this time. Walking around sometimes with thousands of dollars in my pocket, I couldn't not have a strap. I didn't carry it with me a lot, and I didn't want to use it, but the gun was necessary for me to move how I was moving. Otherwise, people would try to take advantage of me. That was one of my first lessons in the concept of leverage—you didn't have to be all crazy with your leverage for it to serve a purpose. Some of my peers liked violence, and I could tell they were looking for any excuse to bust their guns. That was never my mindset. I always felt like there was a better way to handle things. Sometimes the best leverage is just out of sight.

My style elevated after I met an older hustler named Press. He was interested in different things than the ordinary guy on the block. He had money, but a blue-collar car. We'd all be looking at *The Source* magazine, and he was reading the *Robb Report*. Once day he showed up with a bag of loose diamonds, pulled out a loupe, and started talking about cut, color, and clarity. Another time he showed me some jeans I should buy, and when I said they looked dirty, I learned the meaning of clothes with "character." Most guys didn't pick up on this stuff, they were smoking weed or dust or just not interested. I always stayed sober, and Press caught my interest.

Finally my curiosity got the best of me and I asked, "Most guys with your bankroll drive a Cutlass on Daytons, or a Benz. Why are you rolling in a hatchback Honda Civic?"

"Listen," Press said. "If I can't buy the car that I want, I'm not going to spend a lot of money on something else."

"What car do you want?"

He opened up his *Robb Report* and pointed: "This is a Bentley."

In the early 1990s, nobody was talking about Bentleys—not rappers, not ballplayers, nobody. Press flipped to the back of the *Robb Report* and said, "Did you know you can buy an island out of this magazine?"

*Hmmm.* I was seeing something new. This was definitely not just more Cleveland.

. . .

One of our biggest gambling spots was "the Hut." It was located in Forest Hill Park, on property originally bought by John D. Rockefeller in 1873, when he was on his way to becoming the richest man in the world. Rockefeller owned hundreds of acres of land, and he built a mansion in the park to go with the one he had on Millionaires' Row. He lived in Cleveland year-round until he moved to New York City in 1884, but even after that he still spent summers on that Forest Hill estate. The property passed down to his son, John Rockefeller Jr., who in the 1930s donated more than two hundred acres for use as a public park. By the time we came around, the park had a playground, swimming pool, basketball court, and a wooden pavilion that provided protection from the elements. That pavilion was the Hut.

Man, we used to gamble so hard down there. You'd walk down the hill and into the park and see guys playing cards on the benches and shooting dice on the basketball court. The Hut itself was for big money games. The whole scenario was basically an open-air casino.

We never went to the Hut looking bummy. Sometimes my friends and I rode the bus to the mall and bought new outfits, wore them out the store, and went straight to the Hut. Or we got dressed just to stand on the corner outside the store, walk down to the Hut, then walk back to the store and hang out some more. All the while I'm wearing spotless sneakers, crisply ironed jeans, and maybe a Polo rugby shirt and a jacket, maybe Nautica. By the time I got to the eighth grade, I was not afraid to spend an astronomical amount of money on one item of clothing. I still liked Polo, but Press put me up on Versace, Coogi, Iceberg, and Moschino. It was not unusual for me to spend six or seven hundred dollars on a sweater. Two hundred fifty for a T-shirt? Cool. There was a boutique called Cricket West in the Beachwood mall, which was not a place a lot of Black kids went. Cricket West had items the department stores didn't necessarily carry, like Frye boots or belts with the pop bottle caps on them. Most of my peers only focused on the sneakers, like I did back in elementary school with the Jordan 4s. But I had outgrown that way of thinking.

Part of my obsession with clothes was the desire for the status and attention they provided and the way a precise outfit felt like armor against sadness. But that's not the whole picture. Looking back on it now, a lot of it was also about leadership and sophistication. I'm not a follower. I watched my mother follow a drug right into an abyss. I didn't have a lot of choices to make on that set of blocks that defined my young life, but I could choose how I looked. And I chose not to look like everybody else. I was going to have a style that fit who I was as a person. Everything I did, I did a certain way. I didn't want to do anything sloppy in life, so I wasn't going to wear sloppy clothes. I wouldn't be caught in a lesser brand. I'm wearing something you might not know about. Just like the way my grandmother bathed her mother with meticulous care, or my uncle kept himself on military time just to pick up groceries and see his girl, I wanted everything I did to feel conscious and intentional. I wasn't doing anything as noble as caretaking an elder or feeding a family, but all the same: In the wild swirl of my life, I needed to feel like I was moving at my own speed, making choices with intention.

My style also came from a place of respect. When I walked into somebody's house to see their son or their daughter, I wanted my clothes to align with my character, and my character aligned with my respect for others. I wasn't going to wear a long white tee to my knees just because that became the dope-boy uniform one year. No. When I encountered older people in the neighborhood, maybe Miss Givens and her sister, Auntie Net Net, they might say, "You look nice today, Richard." That meant a lot. I didn't want to add to a visual landscape of decay and chaos. I wanted to show up like I cared about myself and my block—and the people who lived on it.

My style also came from a place of preserving my humanity. It came from having clarity within my life when almost no one else seemed to, from having a strong mental structure despite living in a war zone, from having an understanding of how life is actually supposed to be lived. It was a symbol of refusing to submit to all the dumb shit happening around me.

When you have style, people want to know who you are. I'm an eighth grader who doesn't drink, doesn't smoke, I'm not a gangster, I don't sell crack. My fashion became my star power. Before long, in every part of Cleveland, Ohio, when you said, "Little Rich from St. Clair," people responded, "Oh yeah, you talking 'bout the little nigga that can dress." Communicating through style is still part of who I am today. I'll sit courtside at a Lakers game wearing Tom Ford tuxedo pants and a Larry Johnson UNLV jersey underneath a denim jacket. Everyone from movie stars at the game to the fan watching on TV wants to know, "Who is *he*?"

Control is a funny thing.

One reason a lot of people aren't successful is they're trying to control everything but what they can control. Putting energy into what somebody else said, spending all day on Instagram worried about what somebody else has, where they are, what they're doing, who they're doing it with. You don't control any of that, and meanwhile your life is as messy as they come. If you put that energy into what you can control, it creates a better outcome. For thirteen-year-old me, controlling what I could control meant matching the accents on my sneakers to the color of a stripe on my Tommy Hilfiger shirt.

I'm not saying that I thought about all this when I selected an outfit to wear to a park built by a billionaire and now populated by dope boys. But I was starting to sense that there was something else out there, beyond what I could see in Cleveland. When my chance came to grab hold of it, I intended to look the part.

RULE

**Don't Sleep In.**

## 12

## ST. CLAIR

For those who know, Cleveland has always been a town full of gangsters. The Mafia started operating in the city in the early 1900s and rose to national influence. The second *Godfather* movie included a reference to the "Lakeview Road Gang," which was based on a real Mafia family that owned hotels and casinos in Las Vegas and Havana. When my homies and I were kids, we knew about the mob but were more attracted to legendary Black gangsters. We started calling ourselves Crips, but that only lasted a few weeks. Official gang affiliations weren't an organic part of our neighborhood—what mattered was what block you were from.

Some blocks were allies, some were enemies. Carlos was from Ohlman; it was always that one block against everybody else. Holy was from 117th but spent most of his time on 125th, which is the block he claimed. Pill Mil was from Eddy Road but really 125th and St. Clair. I'm from 125th and St. Clair, but could go anywhere. I had a likability factor that eased my path. Everybody recognized me for gambling and dressing fly, and they knew I wasn't about busting guns or robbing anybody. I had jokes and liked to put people at ease. And I knew everybody on every block from playing so many sports. So when I traveled around the neighborhood, no one asked, "Why is he around here?"

The common denominator of all these different blocks was St. Clair Avenue.

St. Clair was a culture. It has always been a famous, well-traveled strip in Cleveland; you can ride it from downtown all the way to Buffalo, New York. When Bone Thugs-N-Harmony released their first album in 1993 they spread St. Clair culture around the world. Dudes from St. Clair had a certain aura about them— a cockiness, a confidence, a "wish a motherfucker would" type of mentality. Everybody in our circles could tell the difference between a St. Clair dude and a guy from Down the Way or from Superior. Even within St. Clair, we could tell the difference between a guy from 79th and a guy from 125th, or between a guy from 117th and a guy from 141st. The tell could be anything from a haircut to a certain posture, but we knew.

St. Clair was the biggest hood in our city, our Crenshaw, our Harlem, our Southwest Atlanta. The rivalries were complex, like with gangs in Los Angeles, where being a Crip didn't mean you got along with every other Crip, and being a Blood didn't mean you got along with every other Blood. The same thing applied to St. Clair. A simple affiliation wasn't enough to guarantee peace. Within St. Clair there were factions: 108th and 117th didn't get along; 101st and 102nd would kill each other, even though you could throw a football from one block to the other. No matter what side you were on, you'd better be aware of your surroundings. Every street was its own nation, and within that nation were smaller conflicting sets. We navigated worlds within worlds. That's just how the hood was.

There were specific stores that people would or would not go to, depending on what block they were from. The same way you don't just walk up into somebody's house, dudes from Brackland Avenue, which was two blocks north, wouldn't necessarily be welcomed in my dad's store. If they did approach, guys standing outside could be like, "Who is you, man? What you doing here?" Then somebody might say, "Oh that's such-and-such's cousin" or "He just moved into what's-his-name's old house," and tensions would ease. Word on the street was like our social media.

On the flip side, some guys from Edmonton have only set foot on Brackland Avenue maybe five times in their life. They've driven down Brackland in a car, but they almost never got out. Let me remind you that Brackland is only two blocks away.

As for me, I was on Brackland all the time. I could go pretty much anywhere. But I was different.

All that said, St. Clair was a family, too. If we were all at a club and 117th got into it with some boys from Kinsman or Harvard, the rest of St. Clair would have our back. Even though we didn't get along Up the Way, in the club we were together. That was the weirdness of it, but in the moment, loyalty to my hood felt instinctual. Cleveland is a tough city, so I can't say St. Clair is the hardest. Kinsman is hard. Harvard is hard. Union, Cedar, Miles, Up the Way, Down the Way, Hough, Wade Park—it's tough all across the board. We just had to hold our own.

Talking shit was an art form for us. Being quick and witty with put-downs and funny comments added to your reputation and made it easier to do whatever you were trying to do on the block. We were merciless with it, too. If you had some kind of visible disability—one eye or one arm—that got talked about. At the same time, you could have the best clothes and a pocket full of money, and a guy with one eye or one arm would light your ass up if you weren't quick-witted enough to defend yourself. If you couldn't talk shit, you couldn't survive. A girl named Joyce was the most dangerous person on the block. She was pigeon-toed and bow-legged, and believe it or not she had buckteeth, too. But Joyce was so funny when she cut guys up, they would just have to walk away. Joyce was a little older than us, and she had a stroke a few years ago that put her in a wheelchair. But she's still funny as hell to this day, cutting people up on Instagram.

I liked to laugh and joke a lot, and I was not afraid to smile. That was natural for me, part of my God-given personality, even though some of my friends felt they had to look serious all the time so they wouldn't appear weak. But I was comfortable being cheerful—that is, I was comfortable once the parameters of a particular environment were clear. Even then, I kept my eyes open. You could never get too comfortable. There were moments when even a cheerful person had to keep an ice grill. A smile was something you had to feel out throughout the day. You had to feel when somebody was in a joking mood, and you had to know the personnel around you to know whether you were in an environment for joking around. But there were times when I had to let all that go and crack a joke because it just needed to be cracked. That's just who I was.

Another thing about St. Clair is that we got up early every morning to get that money. I was accustomed to an early start anyway, because ever since moving into Grandma Johnnie Mae's house, my dad picked me up at five-thirty each morning in his Coupe DeVille so we could open the store at six. But it wasn't just me on those streets at dawn. Listen to Bone Thugs' big hit "First of the Month," and they're talking about *wake up, wake up* . . . Guys hustled before school every day, they got their hair cut before school. On the weekends, guys got up early to hit the mall to buy clothes to wear while they stood out on the block. Breakfast also was a serious thing for us. We'd eat at Will's, Angie's, or Shay's. Shaw Derry was another spot, run by a lady named Ms. Smith. She cooked everything on one little hot plate. I ordered the same thing every time: a sausage egg and cheese sandwich with grape jelly. All

I had to do was call the spot and say who I was—"OK, it'll be ready in ten minutes." That was part of the character of St. Clair, too. We didn't sleep in.

The stereotype of a hustler is that he hustles because he doesn't want to work. That's inaccurate. Hustling was way harder than working a nine-to-five. You had to be up early and out late, pager going off 24/7/365. No weekends off or vacations. Constantly working to perfect your hustle, in terms of how you did business and with whom. The stereotype of the lazy or irresponsible hustler is like the image of athletes as "just playing a game" for a living, which ignores the countless hours of training, practice, studying, handling their business affairs, and *then* having to perform in front of a million people. People see the fruits of a hustler's labors and think it comes easy. Nah, man. Being successful in the streets takes a lot of discipline, hard work, late nights, and early mornings.

. . .

We finished gambling at the Hut and some of us wanted to take the bus to the mall to spend our winnings. I had ridden my tricked-out bike to the park, so I hopped on and started pedaling home to put it away. I rode up the hill out of the park, and when I bent the corner I saw some guys I didn't recognize. The vibe was way off, I could feel them staring. Before I could turn my bike and get away they ran up on me, pushed me off my bike, and took off, one of the guys pedaling away on my prized two-thousand-dollar possession.

I jetted back down to the Hut and got my people. We found them dudes quickly, because they were way out of their element and we knew every inch of our hood, and let's just say we took my bike back. Some fists and kicks were exchanged, threats were made, and we went our separate ways. I took my bike home, grabbed my strap in case the thieves came back, and met back up with the guys for the bus ride to the mall.

We were way across town when the bus stopped, the doors opened—and the guys who jumped me just so happened to get on the bus we were riding.

My homies wanted to set it off then and there. More than a few of us had guns on us. At the very least, guys wanted to follow them off the bus and get at them. I had to explain to my people—*Look, we already beat them down and proved our point. They know we ain't no suckers. Their energy isn't like they want to do something, so why should ours be? I have the most right to be mad out of everybody, because it was my bike they took, and I ain't even mad no more. Starting something with these guys after we already finished it—that just makes no sense. We good.* Respect was established. The streets could be a cold and dangerous place, but I lived by my own code. I just wanted to keep the peace, find a way to come up, and survive.

My friends and I got to the mall and spent our money. Nobody shot anybody that day.

RULE

**Choose the
Best of Everything.**

# 13

# WHAT DISRESPECT IS ABOUT

Glenville High School had legendary status when I was growing up. The school building was in the middle of all the action, on the corner of 113th and St. Clair. My friends and I all wanted to play ball for Glenville, but not because they sent a lot of guys to college or the pros. Glenville was legendary because it was *our* team, the squad that represented our neighborhood. Our older siblings and cousins played there, we grew up attending games with our family members, there was a tradition attached to it. When I was still in middle school I knew older guys on the team and rooted for them. It's like growing up a Browns or Tottenham fan—that's *your* team, win or lose. On Friday nights, high school football games were the biggest thing happening in Cleveland. Glenville played Friday afternoons, though, before it got dark, be-

cause it was so dangerous at night. The atmosphere in the Glenville school building mirrored the streets around it—fights after
school, guns, gangs, drug dealing. It was like that school in the
movie *Lean on Me.* But none of the problems fazed me because I
had already learned to thrive in that environment. I had been looking forward to starting high school at Glenville for years.

At the same time, I knew there were better schools out there,
and I was starting to make a commitment to myself: Even with my
limited choices, I would always choose the best. My cousin Warren
went to University School, and he said they had carpet in their
classrooms. That sounded insane to me. My Uncle John had gone
to Notre Dame–Cathedral Latin. My cousin Tony Miller went to
St. Joseph's and then played basketball at Marquette; my friend
Shayman "Shimmy" Sawyer also went to St. Joe's. We all knew that
Desmond Howard and Clark Kellogg played at St. Joe's before they
made it to the pros. A lot of athletes got recruited to play at Catholic schools, which were considered a step up from a wild place like
Glenville.

Showtime and I played basketball for a Catholic middle school
team, St. Aloysius, coached by Mr. Thornton. I didn't go to school
at St. Aloysius, but they had a rule that if you went to Mass on
Saturday, you could play for the team. I think the Catholic schools
made that exception to scoop up Black athletes. My game developed a lot in middle school. My quickness and jump shot were
elite, to the point where not many grown men in the neighbor-

hood could check me. We played Catholic league games at St. Joseph's, and when I became one of the better players, St. Joe's
started recruiting me. I also got attention from Benedictine, which
was more intriguing to me. My friend Terry who lived across the
street played for Benedictine, and one year his squad went 22–1.
Benedictine turned the lights out when the team was introduced at
home games, like the Chicago Bulls. When I found out the team
shoes were Jordan 9s, sky blue to match the school colors, I was
sold. I was going to Benedictine. To pay the tuition, which might
have been five thousand dollars per year, my dad asked my Uncle
Booker, who worked in the post office, to take out a loan from his
credit union. Dad made the payments. He probably had the cash
on hand but wanted to keep it liquid. I got ready to start the ninth
grade in the fall of 1995.

Grandma Johnnie Mae had me listed as an authorized user on
her credit card for the Dillard's department store. Going into my
freshman year, Dad said I could spend five hundred dollars at Dillard's, and I took my grandma's card to the mall. Benedictine had a
shirt-and-tie dress code, with no sneakers allowed, but I could do
my thing within those rules, and I wanted everything Tommy Hilfiger. I had to have the Tommy shirt, Tommy tie, Tommy belt,
Tommy pants, Tommy socks—multiple versions of each. I loaded
up my shopping cart and pulled up to the register. I was supposed
to stop at five hundred dollars, but when the register finished
counting, it was fifteen hundred.

Dillard's called my grandma to make sure this baby-faced kid wasn't running a scam. "Mrs. Paul, we have a Richard Paul Jr. here, is he authorized to spend fifteen hundred dollars?"

"Hell no!" Grandma said. "Send that boy home!"

I had to get on the phone and explain to her that I had the cash to cover the extra grand. To be honest, I was hoping I wouldn't have to give her the money; I was probably banking on my dad paying the extra or her forgetting about it. But I was going to have that Tommy. I can admit now that I had an addiction to fly clothes. Not just as fashion, but for the feeling they gave me, the affirmation I received from my peers. When you live in a house of pain, that kind of affirmation is like a drug that makes it all feel better. When I was alone, vulnerable, and needed a dependable source of love, where could I get that feeling? From having the new $160 Chris Webber Nikes on my feet, white and navy with the air bubble and Webber's number "2" on the back—and then the next week, having a totally different pair of sneakers. Was it healthy? No. But I never turned to using drugs, no blunts, joints, pills, sherm, none of that. My high was being fly. It wasn't love, but what's love got to do with it?

. . .

Fast-forward about twenty-five years. It's a few weeks before the 2022 NBA All-Star Weekend. I'm sitting in a meeting with Tommy Hilfiger, and he's asking me for advice about his business—what makes brands hot, how young consumers react to different types of marketing, those kinds of things. I went from shopping for Tommy gear, to giving Tommy himself advice about his business. My love of fashion positioned me for a seat at that table. Talk about full circle. It wasn't the money I spent on clothes that got me into that room with Tommy but the attention I paid to fashion, down to the finest detail, with my own creative touches. I didn't just pay attention to the clothes, either. I paid attention to the effect they had on people—the way the older aunties in the hood would smile when they saw me looking clean and sharp on a street full of empty lots, or the way the crowd cheered just a little louder when our team walked onto the court fully coordinated with the latest sneakers. Mindless consumption and running up big bills didn't get me to the table with Tommy. What I cultivated during those years was something more important: careful curation and creativity. As always, it came down to paying attention—which is another way of saying it was about love.

Consulting with Tommy Hilfiger still feels surreal. I hope that young people today, especially kids from disadvantaged backgrounds, can envision the way that applying attention to detail and creativity to the things they love can pay off in the wider world. I couldn't fully see it when I was young, because there were no visible examples. No disrespect whatsoever to Clark Kellogg, but he was as good as it got. If you had told me at age fourteen that I would be in a meeting with Tommy Hilfiger, I would have thought you meant be in a meeting *wearing* Tommy Hilfiger.

. . .

Benedictine was in the middle of a different hood known as Buckeye, on Martin Luther King Jr. Drive, about twenty minutes from my house. Anytime a street is named after Martin Luther King, you know it runs through the ghetto. I didn't have any problems going to and from school, but I definitely kept my head on a swivel. The Benedictine football field was a few blocks away from the school, and sometimes the players had to fight their way back and forth to practice. Even worse, kids from the public middle school up the street, Audubon, liked to rob Benedictine students as they walked to the bus stop. I'm talking about eighth graders taking money and jewelry from high school juniors and seniors. One time a Benedictine kid was riding past Audubon in his car with his arm hanging out to catch the breeze. When he stopped at a light, someone ran up and snatched his watch right off his wrist.

It was calmer inside the school building, which had between three and four hundred students. Benedictine placed a high value on discipline, hard work, humility, and community. We had a huge sports culture, which helped me fit in. The school was all boys, so with no girls around, sports was the main thing that occupied our attention. In 1997 we won state championships in football, basketball, and track. But the school didn't put athletes on a pedestal. No matter how good you were at sports, you had to respect others and work hard in the classroom. Every kid was valued for whatever they brought to the table, whether that was sports, drama, or band.

The school constantly reinforced the message that we were all God's children. It helped that we were one of the few Catholic schools with a Black principal, Mr. Chuck Reynolds. Teachers and coaches talked about being an "M.O.B.," which stood for Man of Benedictine. The school motto was *Ora et Labora*—Pray and Work.

Our student body was about 70 percent white, from a mixture of economic backgrounds. A lot of Cleveland's ethnic white people are Catholic, like the Italians and Irish, and they have strong working-class roots. So we had a lot of blue-collar white kids in our school compared with wealthier private schools like St. Ignatius. Benedictine was more down-to-earth. A small percentage of the Black kids were affluent or middle-class, but most of us came from single-parent homes, or lived with a grandparent like I did.

I decided not to play football in high school. Summer was peak hustling season, and I didn't want to lose all that money to start football practice in August. Also, I wasn't growing. When my freshman year started, I made friends easily, including with white students, but that was nothing new for me because I had interacted with some white friends and schoolmates in St. Louis and at Upson Elementary in Euclid. I immediately connected with another freshman on the basketball team named Mike Woods, from 93rd and Kinsman. Mike's father had been killed by an off-duty cop, and his mom had been sent to prison and then deported to Jamaica. Mike was raised by his grandmother, like me. As a ballplayer, Mike was nasty. He had great pace to his game, long arms, a helluva crossover, could defend, shoot the three, get to the midrange and the rim—he had a complete game. I was the point guard on the freshman team, and Mike ran the two. He became my best friend at Benedictine.

I still opened up the store with my dad at six every morning and worked there after school until about seven-thirty. I noticed that my friends from the neighborhood were coming by the store driving cars, wearing Versace shirts and big-block Mauri gators, talking about dice games and girls. I'm standing there in what felt to me like a sucker outfit, wearing moccasins instead of Jordans. I started to regret going to Benedictine. I was bored. The schoolwork wasn't hard for me, and outside of basketball, there was no excitement. I felt like all the action was passing me by.

I decided to flunk out.

If I got kicked out, I figured, I would be back in the thick of the action at Glenville High. Early during my freshman year I stopped doing any homework and left most of the answers blank on tests.

Everything was going according to plan when one day I was riding with Dad in his Coupe DeVille. Real casually, he asked if I knew the story of what happened to Marvin Gaye.

"Didn't he die of an overdose?" I said.

"No, that's not what happened. His father took him out."

"What you mean, 'took him out'?"

I'll never, ever forget what my dad said next:

"Marvin Gaye's father shot him dead. And the father didn't do a day in jail."

While I digested that piece of information, Dad said, "Your

dean of students, Mr. Tony Russ, sent me your grades. You have a 1.4 GPA. Mr. Russ also told me how well you tested coming into the school. Those tests don't align with your grades. It's obvious you're not applying yourself in class."

Richard Paul Sr. always carried a .38 pistol. He lifted up the armrest and I could see the .38 tucked underneath.

"You keep this up I'm gonna take you out of this world, man. I'm telling you what's going to happen," Dad said. "And I'm not gonna do a day in jail about it. You keep disrespecting me, I'm gonna show you what disrespect gets you. I'll show you what disrespect is about."

That moment changed the trajectory of my life—not all at once, but it is a moment I've replayed a thousand times, from my darkest days to my most decisive crossroads. It's a moment I think about even now. Coming from my dad, I knew the message didn't have much to do with Tony Russ and grades. Dad used the grades as the object lesson because he knew I was tanking and could bring them up. But what he was really explaining to me was that my life mattered. Even if he had to threaten that life to make the point, I got the message. It was the same message he'd been sending me my entire life in a hundred different ways: *If you don't live consciously, you're not going to make it.* The street life that he knew so well, that had entangled his own life in some ways, even as he tried to move away, that is the life he wanted me to escape, before I sank so deep into it that I got lost. I wanted so badly to exercise control in my own life, but he was letting me know that I was in danger of the money, addictive action, and negative energy of the streets controlling me. Once that happens, you find yourself going down a very dark tunnel with no room to turn around and you never come out. All of that was written between the lines of his talk that day in the Coupe.

As a kid, all I wanted was to know that someone cared about me. As I've said, my father and mother, my grandmother, they weren't the kind of people to walk around saying "I love you." That's just not who they were, even though I knew, deep inside, that they genuinely did. But when my dad gave me that talk in his car—that was one moment when I could really feel the love.

Years later, I found out that Dad always told people, "That boy is going to be somebody." It kills me that he never got to see that he was right.

# PART III

# WINS
# AND
# LOSSES

RULE

**Find Your Purpose.**

# 14

# THE VALUE OF BEING HUMBLED

Once Dad scared me straight, I embraced academics, and my GPA never dipped below 3.6. I decided that having the best grades was another way to have the best of everything. I was serious about being on top. I participated in class and asked questions. Math and English were my best subjects. I remember my teachers: Mr. DeGeronimo for math, Mr. Francioli for English, Father Michael who taught theology, Father Dominic for art. The Spanish teacher, Ms. Pymn, might have been the only female teacher at the school, and she wasn't fazed by all the testosterone in the building. "Unpuff that chest," she used to tell us. Our principal, Mr. Reynolds, had graduated from Benedictine decades ago, went to Purdue, and was a great role model. He had no problem telling kids he was the H.N.I.C. White kids had to figure out that meant "head nigger in charge." Mr. Reynolds was in a tough position, because when he disciplined some of the Black students, their parents accused him of being an Uncle Tom. But he didn't care what color the kids were. He handled things the Benedictine way regardless.

While focusing on my books, I still had to be Little Rich. I knew how to work the dress code so that I still stood out, because everything would be top-end Tommy or Polo—shirt, tie, sweater, belt, jacket, pants, all the way to my socks and underwear. All the Black kids sat at the same lunch table, and of course the conversation one day turned to something about playing some cards. That caught my attention, and my man Mike Woods's, too. Turns out he loved to gamble as much as me. After school we found someplace out of the way and got to it. As the game of tunk went on, I started singing the classic Kenny Rogers song "The Gambler": *"You got to know when to hold 'em, know when to fold 'em . . ."* The other guys were confused. They weren't from my neighborhood and didn't really know my rep. Mike's jaw dropped when my bankroll came out my pocket and it was upwards of a thousand dollars. I won and then finished the song: *"You never count your money when you're sittin' at the table / There'll be time enough for countin' when the dealing's done."* Over time, that became one of my trademarks at Benedictine, singing Kenny Rogers while we played tunk.

Mike and I found other ways to bring a little of that hustler spirit to Benedictine. There was a student group in school called the Black Cultural Organization that threw great parties in the school auditorium, and kids from across the city would come.

Freshman year, when the party was coming up, Mike Woods noticed that the tickets were printed on regular plain paper. We hit the copy shop and then sold the tickets we printed for half price to everybody in our neighborhoods. We didn't feel like it was stealing, because the BCO had already sold their tickets out, and their clientele was totally different than ours. Our extra sales put the BCO party on steroids, and the room was packed. Crucial Conflict's song "Hay" was popping then, and when it came on at clubs like Vel's, my crew would get real rowdy, it was that kind of song. It wasn't like you wanted to fight on the dance floor, but to an outsider it might look like a brawl was about to jump off. Well, I had twenty of my guys in the BCO that night, and when "Hay" came on, I pushed it to the limit.

Basketball season started and things were going smoothly on the team. One night we were playing a game at Shaker, and when I was walking out of the locker room at halftime, a girl came up to me and said, "You got my sister pregnant."

I didn't score a single point the next half. I was so shook I could barely dribble. When I worked up the nerve to tell my dad, he said, "Well, that basketball shit is over. You better get a job after school. No son of mine ain't gonna support his child."

I was fourteen. The girl decided not to have the baby, but the close brush with early fatherhood didn't change my ways. I learned a lot of valuable things growing up, but healthy sexual habits were not one of them. Almost everything my friends and I learned about how to approach sex was wrong. First of all, we thought that the more girls you had sex with, the more status you had. You could be dead broke, but if you had a lot of sex, you thought you were winning. It was like a sickness. Guys we looked up to bragged about having a girl on the block, another one around the corner, and a third on the West Side. A girl I was seeing might call me up and inquire about my location and I'd respond, "Don't ask me where I'm at." The girls paid a high price, even those who didn't get pregnant. We were buying them everything, giving them five and six hundred dollars at a time, they had more money than their mothers. I spent so much money on them at McDonald's, they might have run out of Chicken McNuggets. All we were doing was setting up a toxic dynamic that, for some of us, has lasted a lifetime—we saw sex as transactional or a way to show off our status, instead of as an act rooted in love and commitment.

. . .

Like a lot of young kids who play ball, I planned on making it to the NBA. My sophomore year, I didn't make varsity, except for dressing for a few games at the end of the season. Other kids were getting bigger; I wasn't. My size didn't seem like so much of a disadvantage until I got to the varsity level of intensity.

My money wasn't small, though. After school I did my homework and went to practice until six. Then I hit the block until about ten. I started out hustling weed on 125th, Ohlman, and then Brackland. Later, I established myself on 117th and St. Clair, and there was no looking back. I still had the plug, and people started calling my product by my name. Like, "Yo, I'm trying to get some of that Little Rich."

The only issue was that I was still living with Grandma Johnnie Mae and Uncle Charlie, and they both went to bed early. If I wasn't inside the house before they closed up for the night, there was no coming in and out. I never had a key to her house. She told me, "I'm not going to give you a key and you leave it somewhere, then somebody comes in here and knocks me upside the head. When you come in, I'd rather get up and open the door. Not to mention you don't need to be out late anyway."

I had too much respect for my grandma to violate her rules, but I was still immature and caught up in the rapture of making so much money. On some nights when my business kept me out late, I slept on the floor at Uncle Lance's house, where Meco lived. Other times I stayed at my friend Mike Ivey's house on Edmonton, twelve houses down from the store. Mike's mom waitressed at a bar from four in the afternoon until three in the morning, so we had the place pretty much to ourselves. He had a tiny room with a bunk bed, a burgundy sectional sofa, and a floor-model console TV. Mike's mom kept their two-bedroom ground-floor home in immaculate condition, all glass mirrors and white furniture. None of the neighborhood dudes were allowed inside—not for a glass of water, not to use the bathroom, nothing. If she even saw guys sitting on her porch, she'd deliver a stare that felt like a cold gust of wind. But for some reason, Mike's mom took a liking to me and Meco, and we were the only guys allowed to step inside the door.

Mike had great taste in music and was up on a lot of East Coast artists that our neighborhood didn't embrace, like Nas, Mobb Deep, Grand Puba, and Wu-Tang. He was a Notorious B.I.G. fan when most of our friends were Team Tupac. Mike's fashion sense was also different. He'd wear a Florida Panthers or New Jersey Devils jersey before Snoop Dogg made hockey jerseys popular, and pair them with jean shorts or Nautica swim trunks. Then he'd finish the look with moccasins or Adidas Sambas or K-Swiss sneakers with no socks. He was preppy in the jungle, like a lion wearing a bow tie. That wasn't my style, but I respected how fearless Mike was. On Sundays I'd bring a dozen pairs of sneakers over to Mike's house, he'd bring out a dozen pairs, and we'd clean them using a special concoction Mike formulated out of soap and household cleaning products. We had an assembly line going with a toothbrush and everything. Mike's place became a home base for me all the way through high school, and he became like a brother to Meco and me.

After school, in between making my weed rounds, I might go to the dice house, depending on whether I had a basketball game or not. I was raking in thousands of dollars every week, which I kept in shoeboxes in my little bedroom at my grandmother's house. I didn't open my first bank account until I was nineteen years old.

Around my way, street guys had all the cachet and credibility, not basketball players. The athlete who came closest was my guy Kirky, who had played on Cleveland State's 1986 tournament team. I liked Kirky, he was family, but street guys thought he was corny. As my hustles increased, my incentive to work on my hoop game decreased.

I thought to myself, *You can't take time away from basketball to hustle and think you're going to be a pro. Plus you're short, with small hands. So now what?*

I stayed on the team and was a solid contributor, but I got by on what talent I had, rather than all-out dedication. Our team was excellent my sophomore and junior years and won back-to-back state championships, and we made the championship game my senior year. My jump shot was still money, and I contributed as a shooter off the bench. I started a game here and there, and was fine with being a sub. I enjoyed the team atmosphere, the camaraderie, the feeling of helping guys come together to accomplish big things. Every game was packed, home and away. My teammates were stars on the court but I never felt envious. We all had our lanes. I was a star in a different sky.

It hurt at the time, but there was so much value for me in loving basketball and, eventually, being humbled by it. When I played in local leagues and on junior varsity, I'd been a star on the court, and I felt that glow—I had even let myself dream of taking my talents all the way to the NBA. But there was a moment when it hit me, hard, that for all of my love of the game, I just didn't have the physical gifts and skill that some of my peers did. It was a big bucket of cold water, especially since I always prided myself on being the best at whatever I tried. But I gained such a valuable lesson about finding my purpose. I found real joy coming in off the bench, making my contributions as a role player, practicing hard, and celebrating success with my teammates. I also learned that my ultimate value didn't hinge on whether I was the star player on the team. I was more than that.

All of those lessons keep paying off now. Now I have to help guys in the league who used to be stars, but can't let go of their ego and accept a new role. Then there are my young clients coming into the NBA; every one of them was once the star on their high school or college team, but in truth only a few of them will be the best player on an NBA team, let alone the best in the whole league. But they still need to work just as hard as the best player, maybe harder. I know what it means to wake up at six in the morning and get up extra shots in the gym with my guys. I know about standing on the edge of the steps and doing toe raises to increase my vertical jump, about playing pickup and holding down the court. Star or not, and even after my focus shifted, I practiced hard. I didn't let the streets come before my commitment to myself and my teammates at Benedictine.

But when it was time for summer league, my priorities got clarified.

Summer is different on the block. Everything is elevated, both the stakes and the rewards. My basketball game might start at six, but I'm at the dice game from noon to five-thirty. Depending on how much I'm up or down, maybe I go to summer league, maybe I don't get there exactly on time. I might be down a thousand or fifteen hundred, go play summer league, run back to the dice game and win my money back. I had days like that.

Even though I'd be pissed at myself for being late to my basketball game, that's when I really knew: *Playing basketball ain't what I really love anyway.* I was in love with a different game. You know what I'm saying? Sports shaped me in so many ways, but I was still trying to find my path. I found my truest self in the moments of stress and high stakes, when I had to draw on everything I'd learned—not just skills, but what I'd learned about poise, managing risk, navigating the treachery of the hood with integrity. These are the reasons why winning at a dice game felt more rewarding than winning a basketball game. I could score points in basketball and receive praise, or I could hit points on the dice and get paper. With that paper came freedom, independence, a sense of power and control. When I played games where I felt all those parts of myself engaged, I felt the most alive. In those games, I wanted to be the MVP.

RULE

**Neutralize Your Anger.**

## 15

## THOSE OTHER DAYS

My friend Duck came through the store looking super bummy. Duck had started hustling, especially gambling, at a young age, and on this day I suspected he might have lost all his money after a marathon session. Duck was usually very particular about his appearance, so he was way out of character.

"The hell you looking all crusty for?" Dad said. "This don't even look like you."

"Aww, Mr. Paul, I'm just going through something right now," Duck said.

"I don't care what you going through. You always got to keep yourself presentable, because you never know when an opportunity will arrive. Now go clean yourself up."

Another time Mike Ivey was out front of the store talking to this bowlegged light-skinned girl. She got wild and told Mike, "I'll throw you down and ride your face!" Mike was tripping because no girl had ever talked crazy to him like that. He came in the store geeked up about the situation.

Dad gave him a look and said, "Don't mess with her. She got something."

He was a father to pretty much the whole neighborhood. Closer to home was my brother, Meco. Meco is not my father's son. But to this day, some of our closest friends have been shocked to learn that my brother's last name is not Paul.

When my father died, Meco tatted RICHARD PAUL SENIOR on his arm. The name of Meco's biological father is nowhere to be found on his body.

. . .

Growing up, we used to rank on people. "Ranking" has a lot of regional and generational variations: *joning, snapping, playing the dozens,* whatever. You make fun of someone to the point where everybody laughs at them. It was one of my specialties. Sometimes you're ranking and everything is cool until you go on a run of really funny snaps and the opponent feels like they got to hit you with a low blow. One day I was going off on this guy and had all our friends in stitches. Bro looked like he was about to cry. All of a sudden he said:

"That's why your mother smokes crack."

That threw me off. I tried to act like it didn't matter and kept ranking, but the momentum had shifted. I was scrambling to get off the mat like a boxer who just caught a kidney shot. The same thing happened a couple more times—I'd be in a groove and my opponent would respond with "That's why your mom's a dope fiend," and that put me on my heels.

I started thinking about the scenario when I was alone. My presentation and my rep were important to me, they were part of the credibility I needed to move like I was moving. What it boiled down to, although I didn't recognize it at that young age, was respect. I needed to be respected to be successful.

I turned the ranking situation over and over in my mind until I figured it out. The next time someone joked about my mother, I said:

"You know what? You right, my mom smokes crack. But judging by the way I look and the way you look"—and I paused to let everybody take in my thousand-dollar outfit—"nobody can tell."

The cipher went crazy when I said that. See, I figured out that when someone tried to use my mom's addiction against me, I had three choices: fight; put my head down and brush it off; or come back and make them look stupid by not allowing their best punch to affect me in any way. When I started using the third option, it neutralized the joke, so guys left my mom alone. I learned not to let it hurt me when people called out my mother's struggles. Or even if it did hurt me, I learned not to let it show, not to let it make me act outside of myself. I had to be above it.

If you've trained yourself to stay on your square when someone is talking about your mother, you're on your way to mastering self-discipline. Nowadays, when people want to spread gossip about me as an agent or throw dirt on Klutch, which happens a lot in this business, I put that same self-discipline into practice. You're not going to make me react to anything. If I could control myself when some kid called my mother a crack fiend, then I have no problem dealing with slander from haters and competitors trying to bring me down in business. And the best way to deal with it is to stay calm and think for a moment, so you have the distance to consider whether the slander is a real threat or should just be ignored. If you decide it is a threat: Counterattack on your own terms, in your own way, in your own time. Never respond on someone else's terms and timetable. Never react with your own first reflex in a moment of rage or embarrassment.

Growing up, I saw impulsive decisions get so many people sent to jail or killed. You can't have trigger points when you live in the ghetto, you just can't, because that gives anyone the power to knock you off your square. Suppose someone says, "That's why your mama's a bitch." Now I got two choices: fight, or take the high road—for now. If I choose to fight based upon words, I might be killed. I might have to kill. Those were the stakes when I was a young teenager.

My dad used to make me watch *The Godfather* with him. He had it on tape and played it all the time. I thought it was boring at first, but when I started understanding the nuances and psychology behind everything, it taught me a lot, which was my dad's intent. Me reacting to someone calling my mama a crackhead or a bitch is Sonny Corleone getting killed at the causeway because his sister's husband beat her. Barzini knew Sonny was a hothead, he knew how Sonny would react, and he used that to trap and kill him.

This is how I processed my mother's struggles with addiction. To carry that in public, I had to wear my emotional armor. The armor was what I presented to the world, but underneath, of course, it hurt when someone said my mom was a crackhead. It hurt mostly because I knew the truth in the statement: She was, in fact, addicted to crack. I couldn't deny or sidestep that, but I had to bury the pain it caused me. I couldn't show any feeling, because that would put me in danger. I even hid it from myself, while it ate me up from the inside.

I also had to remember that while it was true she was an addict, it wasn't the whole truth about who she was. I held on to who my mom was when she wasn't getting high. Like my dad had explained to us, it's a sickness, so in my mind, her being called an addict wasn't inherently derogatory. The real ignorance came from the person who would talk down about somebody who is sick. It was no different than making fun of my Aunt San because she had Down's syndrome.

I held tight to the good memories of my mother. She could be amazing, vibrant, energy off the charts, loving, caring. Everybody enjoyed being around her. Children loved her. She would give you the shirt off her back. I thought back to her cooking up shrimp in our apartment above the store, singing along to "Woman's Gotta Have It" by Bobby Womack, and remembered how warm and safe I felt.

Then there were those other days.

. . .

I dipped by the store to try and catch Dad before he closed up. I was sixteen, driving my first car, a 1986 Buick Skylark with a messed-up carburetor. My girlfriend at the time was in the passenger seat; in the back were her friend and her cousin. I pulled up and saw that the door to the store was locked, but I heard arguing from inside. I'm trying to figure out what's going on when a guy standing outside the store says, "Your mom and dad in there fighting."

Something broke inside me.

I was just done with it, done with everything: the craziness and drama, the void where my mother should have been, the pain of her absence, the different pain of her presence. I was done with it all. I banged on the door and yelled as loud as I could. "Open up, it's Rich! Open this fucking door!"

Dad opened the door, the same door that my mom walked through years earlier for the first time when she met him. I barged inside. Dad stood there with a calm face, but I could tell he was upset. It was the closest I ever saw him to not being in control. Mom had that "wish a nigga would" look in her eyes.

I told her, "We're not doing this, Mom. We're not doing this. What do you want?"

"What you mean we ain't doing this?"

"This, Mom. All this yelling and screaming. You ain't about to be tearing shit up in here. Now what do you want?"

"I need some money but this motherfucker"—she cut her eyes at Dad—"is acting brand-new."

I went in my pocket and peeled off a couple hundred. "Here, Mom. Now quiet down and be on your way. I don't want to see you back here acting like this no more."

For a moment I didn't know what was going to happen. I was ready for anything. Dad's eyes were wider than I had ever seen them.

And then Peaches put the money in her pocket and walked out of the store.

A lot changed in that moment: The relationship between me and my mother, how my father saw me, my feelings about our family. Something broke that could never be repaired, even after my mom got better.

When you see your mother walk away holding tighter to some bills than she ever held on to you, it's hard to trust anyone after that.

RULE

**Learn the Art of Bearing
Down and Letting Up.**

## 16

# GOTTA BE THE ONE

Something in me broke that day when I was sixteen, but the years before might have fooled me into thinking I was unbreakable. I grew up a whole lot from twelve to sixteen. I got myself into a prestigious high school that offered a pathway to college. I thought I'd figured out how to keep my mom's addiction from driving me crazy. I started a weed business that provided a steady source of income, and became a good enough dice shooter to compete in the big neighborhood games. I became *that nigga* among my young friends.

After my run-in with my mother at my father's store, I changed. I thought it was for the better. It wasn't enough to just be in the game anymore. Now I needed to be *that nigga,* period. I needed the whole city to know my name. It was more than just my normal competitive urges. The need to win—at everything—became a dangerous obsession.

It all came back to dice. By now, I had mastered the art of throwing dice so in my mind, they would land how I wanted them to land. I could keep the same number coming up almost every time. I had a technique: First of all, when I picked up the dice to shoot, I didn't just grab them any which way. I lined up the numbers according to what I needed, without even looking at them, just based on the feel of the dice in my right hand. Let's say I wanted to roll an eight—I could manipulate the dice to start my roll with both fours on top. That meant fives and twos were on the outside, a pair of threes on the bottom, pair of sixes and pair of ones next to the fours. Got that?

Now when I shake the dice, I make them rattle in my hand without changing position. Then I decide how to roll them, depending on what number I need to hit and what surface I'm on. Carpet is softer than concrete, the dice don't move around as much. If you get a consistent velocity, the dice will tumble in unison, and the odds of winning are better. The roll you use influences the outcome, too. When I put one die on top the other, that roll is called the "Hudson." You flip your wrist back and spin out the dice so they land softly and the top side stays up. Rolling the dice side by side is called the "pad roll." No matter how expertly you roll, the outcome isn't certain, but with the right techniques, the odds are better. When I'm hot I can call my own shot, like a basketball player calls bank or swish. You know how an amateur jangles the dice around in his hand and throws them with no purpose? We call that the "Hully Gully." That's just banking on pure luck, no strategy or skill. Sometimes I shot dice so well, guys refused to bet me unless I rolled Hully Gully.

All of my techniques were acceptable in a street dice game. Things move quickly, so there's no time for anyone to say anything about my technique before the dice come out of my hand. It's not cheating; it's skill. The dice ain't loaded. Just like LeBron or Kobe put in the work in the gym, I practiced my craft and put in work with the dice.

Shooting dice has a lot in common with sports, there's an energy and a flow that you can ride to victory. When a basketball player is in the zone and can't miss a shot and is talking his shit to the other players and to the crowd—the same thing happens in a dice game.

When I'm winning, I have to bear down. That's the discipline I brought to it. If I beat you out of twenty-five hundred and you ain't got but a hundred left, bearing down to get that last hundred is a must. That's the difference between a gambler and a hustler. I ain't no gambler. Gamblers go to Vegas and lose because the odds are rigged against them. Vegas kicks out the hustlers because Vegas can't beat them. Bearing down on that last hundred is about being able to lock in and not get distracted. It's a mental thing. I also want the other guy to understand that he can never beat me. I want him to come back and challenge me, but when he does, I also want him to walk in the door knowing that he's probably not going to win.

After winning, the challenge is holding on to the money. In the circles I gambled in, we were all young guys, trying to get the money and safely get up out of the spot. When we were winning big, we had to tuck. Showing your bankroll was a dangerous thing to do—the walls have eyes, and ears. I could be up three or four thousand, but only show seven hundred in my hand. The rest I tucked away in my pocket when nobody was looking. We used to call ourselves the tuck masters. Another technique was to look at my pager, say I needed to go make a call, then disappear and not come back. We didn't want anybody to get any strong-arm ideas, or to try and borrow money knowing they won't pay you back. Or word might get out that you won big and now everybody is asking for a loan—no sir.

Let's say you're gambling with somebody you know is dangerous and a sore loser. You beat them out of, say, ten thousand. The smart thing to do is give them fifteen hundred. Just give it to them, no strings attached, and leave. That keeps them gambling, and you're gone. You just took all their money. You don't need it to be a thing between you, nor do you want it to be a thing. But as a gentleman, you say, "I got you for ten thousand, here go fifteen hundred. Shoot, here go twenty-five hundred." We call that giving someone a "gapper." That's what the OGs like Wink and Willie Wild taught us to do, and what my dad helped me understand about embracing competition but winning with class and integrity. You might give someone a gapper and they win all their money back with it, then they shoot you back the gapper plus more on top of it.

But some guys might still try to step to you, and then you have to hold your ground: "Well shit man, give me my money back then." You can't be a pushover.

There was never a place that we didn't gamble. Every block was its own casino in one way or another, be it cards, dice, or the Street Fighter video game. Walk into the Glenville Rec Center, go to the back of the locker room—twenty guys are in a huge dice game. My partner Duck, who went to Glenville High School, used to pay the study hall teacher to go get them a meal, and Duck would host a dice game and a card game in the classroom. Duck gambled *and* collected 10 percent of every roll as the guy running the game. So if a guy wins a thousand dollars, he's gotta pay Duck a hundred. Plus Duck could shoot with the best of them. Duck and I gambled side by side in a whole lot of games, and we're still tight to this day.

At this point I wasn't satisfied just having the best clothes. I needed to have things that nobody else could get, even if they wanted to. I started going to every sneaker store and asking for the date when new releases would arrive. This is before you could buy shoes on the internet. After they told me the release date, I negotiated to buy a number of pairs early, for an extra fee that went into their pocket. I told the people who worked in the store, "Look, we're all going to be happy with this arrangement. You're making extra money, you're selling shoes quicker, and I get what I'm looking for." I might go to five stores, and at two of them salespeople would be down with the plan, which was great. I bought a bunch of shoes early, sold some to my friends, and then we all went to Foot Locker the day of the release. A long line of people would be waiting to buy the new Jordans or Barkleys—and we walked up with the shoes already on our feet.

As far back as I can remember, my wardrobe always included sports jerseys, even before they were popular. The first one I remember buying was in '93, when I got the Charles Barkley sneakers and the authentic Phoenix Suns jersey to go with them. Nike brought out another pair of shoes that were green and gold with an air bubble—I wore those with a Shawn Kemp SuperSonics jersey. In the ninth grade, a girl I was seeing asked what I wanted for my birthday, and I asked her for Marshall Faulk's jersey from the Colts. My Spanish teacher, Ms. Pymn, asked if I could get her the jersey of her favorite player, Joe Namath of the New York Jets. I sold it to her for twenty-five bucks, way less than wholesale. That was just smart business.

We were clowning around at the lunch table when Mike Woods's uncle walked up to us. He didn't work at the school and had no business being in the lunchroom, but there he was, wearing a suit and looking nervous.

"Hey Mike," he said, "I need you to pee for me real quick."

"You need me to what?" Mike said. The rest of us were just as confused.

"I have a job interview, and they're gonna give me a drug test," his uncle said. "I need you to give me some clean pee."

We all looked at each other, then back at Mike.

"Man, I wish I could help you, Unc. But if I pee for you, you ain't gonna get the job, you know what I'm saying?"

I knew what Mike was saying. He liked to burn a blunt or two.

"Rich is the only one at this table who can pee for you," Mike said. Everybody knew I didn't smoke or drink.

Mike's uncle looked at me. I put out my hand. He handed me a vial, I took it to the bathroom, filled it up, and returned it to him. Mike's uncle walked out and we went back to clowning around at the lunch table.

. . .

I made great friends at Benedictine, but also moved deeper into an entirely separate life. I still had my guys from the neighborhood, like Showtime, Mike Ivey, and Duck. I started rolling with other neighborhood hustlers my age, like Mike E, Al, and Max. I also hung tight with OGs on different blocks: Wink, Willie Wild, Arms, Donny Dow, Tex, and other guys who gambled every day. OG Mo would come down the street in his candy-blue Cutlass on Daytons, see me on the block and say, "Come ride with me, Rich." All of us were getting money and dressing fly.

My hustling career had begun on 125th, on the corners of Ohlman and then Brackland; 125th will always be my point of origin, and my legacy. On Brackland, my dudes were Dre and Pook. On Ohlman, my older homies were Mont B, who resembled Biggie Smalls after he went from ashy to classy, and Dell Bell. They were best friends with Big Head Boo, who was the older brother of my Muny League football teammate 2 Los. It was all interwoven. Then I moved my hustle to 117th and St. Clair, where my cousin Chaz was the guy, along with Chase, Heavy, and Dext. I still stayed tight with 125th. But you could catch me anywhere around Glenville, and sometimes beyond, hanging with like-minded friends, known in every club and on every strip. Now, 105th was its own world— talk about some money-getting dudes. Hough and Wade Park were not to be played with, they were more low-key but also got a ton of money on the low. I was affiliated with 117th and 125th, but when they had beef with other blocks and neighborhoods, I was carved out of the disputes because I treated everyone with respect. My principles didn't change based on where you were from, so I stayed solid across the town.

I hung with so many different sets of people, I was like air traffic control or central intelligence. When it came to what was happening on the streets, I was connected to everybody. If I took Candace to the movies, I'd see about fifty people I knew at the theater, and I conversated with all of them. It got to the point where Candace got frustrated, because I spoke to so many people that we'd miss the start of the flick.

My sophomore year in high school, Jay-Z dropped his debut

album, *Reasonable Doubt*. Believe it or not, most of my peers weren't feeling Jay-Z at that time. The character of Cleveland is a combination of Midwest and down South, because so many of our ancestors came from Southern states to find factory work. Cleveland was early to embrace the New Orleans sound of Master P and Cash Money. Our first hometown rappers to blow up were Bone Thugs-N-Harmony, who had a unique Midwest sound and style that was particular to their block on East 99th. The Bone Thugs aesthetic didn't apply to Cleveland as a whole; their world was twenty-five blocks from us and totally different from how we were living. So if you took thirty guys from St. Clair, maybe five liked Jay-Z early in his career.

My first reaction to Jay was "This is the life I'm living. This guy is telling my story, but from the perspective of somebody who has achieved everything I'm trying to accomplish." *Y'all feel a nigga's struggle, y'all think a nigga love to / Hustle behind the wheel, trying to escape my trouble* . . . I felt like Jay's words were the map of where I needed to go. I always had an affinity for people who did things in a certain way, who moved with precision, integrity, and confidence. That was Jay. At the time, I saw Jay's map as a guide for hustlers, street dudes, whatever you want to call us. As a teenager, listening to "Politics as Usual"—*The game changes like my mind just ain't right / Rewind get this dough, I guess it ain't your night*—all I saw was the money.

We lived in a dangerous world, but I was able to float above the violence because that wasn't in my nature. I would defend myself,

sure, but everybody knew I wasn't trying to hurt nobody. My reputation was for being a guy who got money and might get you some,
too. But one of the biggest things that kept me safe was Meco.

By this time, my brother was one of the most feared people
from St. Clair. No one wanted to cross him. Meco had a low toler-
ance for anything that deviated from his principles of right and
wrong, and at the top of his list of principles was loyalty. Being
three years older than me, he ran with his own set of dudes, but we
were still super close and everybody knew it. Meco understood
that I never bothered anybody, outside of beating them out of their
money fair and square in a dice game. So if Meco even got wind of
any threat or friction coming my way, he was liable to pull up out
of nowhere and . . . well, I'll just leave that where it is. Sometimes
I hid friction from Meco, because I knew he would go to the extreme. One time we were playing pickup basketball at Glenville
Rec and this grown man punched me in my face because he was
mad I didn't choose him for my team when I had next game. Meco
is salty to this day that I never told him about that. He's not built to
let anything slide. That's a major reason why very few people ever
tried to take advantage of me in the streets.

Meco looked at me one day and said, "Bro, you gotta be the
one."

"What you mean?" I asked.

"I'm doomed, bro. Ain't no telling what I'm out here doing. It
don't end well for niggas like me. But you different, bro."

Meco has surprisingly gentle eyes for a man with his history. He locked those doe eyes on me and said:

"I ain't letting nothing happen to you, bro. You gotta be the one."

. . .

Going to school at Benedictine was a break from the madness. Outside school, the streets I walked were full of pressure and danger, although like so many other Black kids I just internalized it and took it as my normal day-to-day existence. But that type of pressure takes a toll on your mental and physical health, which is one reason why Black men have the shortest average life span of anyone in this country. Benedictine was a safe and positive space. I felt a responsibility and sense of expectation there. Teachers wouldn't allow kids to just sleep their way through class, or pass them just to move them along. You had to earn it. There was competition among the students over grades. Our basketball team probably had a cumulative GPA of 3.6 or 3.7; even the best players were at that level. That is almost unheard of for a majority Black championship team, because so many schools don't care about academic performance when their athletes are winning.

My teachers and classmates probably assumed I would go to college and get a decent job. I always believed I would be successful, too, but my concept of success was shaped by my environment back at home, not by the expectations of my school. A wife, two kids, a dog, a good job, going out to dinner every other Friday, taking two vacations a year, that was what people at Benedictine wanted me to aspire to. I still consider that to be very successful, because it provides peace of mind and a loving family. But everybody's journey is different, and I suspected that wouldn't be mine.

None of my teachers knew about my street life, but some of my classmates did. I didn't hide or compartmentalize that part of me. I carried St. Clair on me heavy, every day. I lived with the same demeanor and edge.

Dad wasn't stupid, he knew I was selling weed and gambling. I never got the sense that he wanted to stop my flow. The world that I'm in today, Dad could never see. It wasn't like he could tell me, *Son, you could be an executive at Apple, or a designer at Nike. You could create an Amazon like Jeff Bezos or start a private equity firm like Robert Smith.* All he tried to do was shape the best hustler and entrepreneur he could, and hopefully, instead of owning a corner store one day, I might own something like a grocery store.

Also, when Dad was my age, he was doing the same things I was doing. That's why he knew he couldn't stop my flow; he just wanted to monitor it. "Be careful," is what he told me. "I'm not going to be here forever. You gotta know where to draw the line. Because if you get in too deep"—and by that he meant selling cocaine, robbing and shooting, and losing control like a lot of young men in our neighborhood were—"there's only two ways out. Dead or in jail.

"You hear me, son? Only two ways out. Dead or in jail."

I took his advice. I wasn't going to leave the streets, but I was going to be as smart as I could be on them, so I strategized and observed. I thought about who to stay away from and who I could trust. I always try to see beyond the surface, to discern the character of people, judge their reliability. I honed that skill as much as I could because it was the only thing that could separate me from everyone else in the game, no matter how street-smart they were. I needed to be smarter. I wasn't going to quit, so I had to maximize my wits and intuition to survive. And just like Dad said, I needed to know where to draw the line.

Some cats used to get heated with me because I wouldn't hustle with them. By the end of high school I could move more than dub sacks of weed. I could supply other dealers. If you needed ounces, or even pounds—holla. But I kept my radar up. When certain guys checked for me I'd say, "I don't know what you're talking about. You must have me mixed up with somebody else." I just had a feeling about them.

One of the toughest decisions I had to make was to not do business with one of my closest friends. We were close, but where I was cagey and moved carefully, he was wild, drinking heavy and hanging out with guys I didn't want anywhere near what I was doing. I knew my friend would take a bullet or shoot a bullet for me, but I also knew that he could unintentionally put both of us in harm's way. So I iced him out.

In business today, I have to use those same skills and awareness.

The product is the only difference, because the product we had easiest access to back in the day was illegal. That illegal commodity was also the only thing we saw that could radically change our circumstances. The legal commodities that the system permitted people like my dad to sell—milk, eggs, cigarettes, beer, lottery tickets, Chore Boys for smoking crack—none of that could change your life. The only business transactions that came even close to the level of business I'm at today were illegal—and working with them was a fast track to jail or the morgue. Working in high-stakes business like that as a kid prepared me to work with some of the people I encounter in legal business today, who will metaphorically cut your throat in a second. The other difference: On the block, you knew when the danger was coming. In the business world, it's harder to see who's trying to kill you.

RULE

**Cheating Will Get You Killed.**

# 17

# THE PRICE OF THE CHASE

The door to the store swung open and Meco rushed inside with two cops right behind him. They caught him and everyone started tussling and fighting. Meco got thrown to the ground and one cop hit him in the face with a flashlight. All of this happened within about five seconds.

Dad jumped up from behind the counter. He had a pistol in each hand.

"Ain't gonna be no fucking Rodney King in here!" he shouted. "That's my son!"

We could never just relax. My muscles and nerves were always on alert for the worst. I'm still waiting for that tension to disappear for good.

. . .

After my first car, the Skylark, I drove an '86 Chevy Cavalier with no reverse. Sometimes during those cold Cleveland winters, I'd start the Cavalier in the morning and go back inside for ten or twenty minutes, so when it was time to leave I'd be warm. I could have afforded a better ride, but an expensive car drew attention and could make me a target of both the police and anybody looking for a come up. Rolling in a who-ride was the smarter option. Like Jay-Z said on "Coming of Age": *You let them other niggas get the name, skip the fame / Ten thou' or a hundred G keep your shit the same.*

That Cavalier was the car I used to make my rounds after school, selling weed. When school or practice was over, I'd have dozens of missed pages on my beeper. Sometimes I let people know to meet me at a certain block, and when I pulled up, there would already be a line of customers, a line of grown men, ten or twelve deep, waiting on those sacks of Little Rich.

I resisted a lot of opportunities to graduate from selling weed to harder drugs. Things were dangerous enough. I heard gunfire every night. I didn't carry a gun to school, but every night when I came home from whatever I was doing, I was strapped for sure. I saw distribution and consumption of crack cocaine every single day. Thanksgiving, Christmas, Martin Luther King Jr. Day, Mother's Day—it never stopped. Never. I saw robberies, pimping and prostitution, shootings, gangsters and killers doing what they do.

Meanwhile, my mom was maneuvering through those same streets. I caught a glimpse of her here and there, gave her money and kept it moving. I was on blocks where literally a hundred guys were outside, most of them carrying guns. I saw every kind of hustle, con, and game being run. Still, I felt protected. I'm pretty sure there were several times that something hostile was coming my way on different blocks and some guys would intervene like, "Nah, Rich is my people." I could feel that energy as I moved around. A few guys probably didn't like me because of the things I had, but I didn't have any real enemies because I treated everyone with respect. It was almost like I was one of those young athletes who the hood protects because he has a future. If something was about to jump off, guys would say, "Yo, leave Rich alone. Go on, Kid, get up outta here."

One afternoon when I was sixteen years old, I won a nice piece of money shooting dice off this dude named Sleepy. After the game we were at the store and Sleepy was talking shit to me and Dad about the money. Sleepy was in his early twenties, in and out of jail. Dad had known him, his parents, and his grandparents for years. After a while, Dad had had enough and said, "We can just lock the door then and get back to it."

"Bet," Sleepy said.

My dad locked the front door and the three of us started shooting dice right there on the floor. We started at fifty dollars a roll, then went to a hundred. My bank stayed about even but Dad was winning big. After a while, it was just Dad and Sleepy going at it for five hundred a throw. After about two hours, Dad got hot and Sleepy went broke.

I don't remember how much Sleepy lost, but it was all he had. No matter if it's two dollars or two thousand, when you take everything from somebody, it cuts deep.

Sleepy was angry and talking about how he got cheated. He stormed out of the store. Dad and I went on with our day.

I was up the block later when I saw Sleepy return to the front of the store. He walked back and forth loud-talking until Dad came out. It was well known that Sleepy had an Uzi, and sure enough, all of a sudden the machine gun was in his hand.

Dad played it cool. I walked over, not too fast because I didn't want to startle a dude holding an Uzi. Dad was talking calmly to Sleepy, friendly and joking but serious, if you know what I mean.

"My man, you lost fair and square," Dad said with a smile. "Now get the fuck outta here with that Uzi."

After a while, Sleepy became apologetic: "Yo, I'm bugging. I'm tripping." He put his Uzi away and went home.

The image of Sleepy with that steel in his hand, staring down my dad, didn't leave me for days.

For me, street life had become about gamesmanship and chasing the thrill of high-stakes competition. Winning felt addictive. But the thrill of victory could quickly be followed by an Uzi in your face. I started to wonder if that kind of winning was winning at all.

Another time I was shooting dice at the Hut with a guy we called Cactus. It was early winter and there was snow on the ground. The clocks had just been pushed back for daylight savings, so it got dark early. The weather and the time change combined to form a gloomy, weird vibe. I beat Cactus out of about three thousand dollars and the game ended. Normally I would have shot him a gapper, but the energy felt off so I just left the game and started walking down Thornhill Drive back to the store. When I looked over my shoulder, I saw Cactus behind me. We had grown up in the same hood, played football and basketball together, he bought plenty weed off me. Cactus was a guy I said what up to every day. Still, my Spidey-senses were jangling. I calculated how far I was from Arlington, where more people would be out and about.

Before I could get there, Cactus rushed up on me and started grabbing and clawing at the pocket of my sweats where the money was. Cactus was about six-foot-three and wide. We tussled all the way down the block until we got to the corner, where he calmed down a little bit.

I was like, "Man, what is wrong with you?"

"That was my last," Cactus responded. I had taken all his money.

I thought about how my father always told me, *If somebody tries to do something bad to you, it's not about you, it's about them.*

I took the high road. Don't go wild about it, be mild about it— that was the choice I made. "You don't gotta rob nobody, man," I said. "All you had to do is ask. I don't care about the money like that. I've known you since kindergarten. Tell me 'I just had a baby' or 'That's my re-up' or whatever the case may be."

"I feel you, Rich. My bad."

I couldn't show weakness, though. I told him, "I ain't giving you all your money back, because I beat you fair and square. You shouldn't be betting against me anyway."

I peeled off fifteen hundred and told him, "Get back on your feet and pay me back when you can."

Cactus took the money, but our relationship was never the same. He paid me back like a cow shits in the road—a drop at a time. I never got all fifteen hundred back. I knew that if he could have gotten away with robbing me, he would have. If it was some-one he didn't really know, he might have killed him for that money. He might have even killed me, if he thought nobody would find out.

Cactus is locked up now. A guy was trying to stick him up, and he took the gun and killed the guy in self-defense. He should have taken the deal the prosecutor offered him, seven or eight years, but he fought the case and got seventeen. When he asked for help sending his son to a better school, I contributed. Yes, he had tried to rob me. But we had been friends since kindergarten.

For every robbery I avoided, I saw five other people get got. We had a term for guys who would rob, lie, and steal and were always scheming: "slept rock." I never wanted to be a slept rock with no integrity, who would do anything to anybody for any reason. I wanted to do right, even within the wrong of my path in life. I knew gambling and selling weed were dangerous and could have bad consequences, but hustling was in my veins. If there was a right way to hustle, that's how I would do it. I credit my dad for that approach, because he both gave and demanded respect. He taught me the meaning of "heart." He radiated integrity and being a stand-up guy through and through. If I acted any other way, I wouldn't be able to sleep at night.

In my business today, some agents go to drastic measures to sign clients, lying about and degrading us. Some agents do that at a very high level, and hide behind the idea that these are the normal words of this business. It's like they're fouling me, then crying to the refs that they're innocent.

The only game with no referees is the streets. That's where I learned the meaning of integrity.

"Never cheat, because that will get you killed," my dad told me. I didn't want to get killed for being a slept rock.

RULE

**Transitions Require
Decisions.**

## 18

# STREETS STILL CALLING

Senior year in high school I rocked herringbone chains, platinum Cartier frames, and a different leather jacket every other week. I had every Jordan sneaker, every Griffey, every Penny, every Barkley. I was taking girls to restaurants and spending hundreds on a meal. I wore Versace, Coogi, Moschino, and Donna Karan, along with my longtime favorites Tommy and Ralph. I liked to wear the big-block Mauri gators with a Versace shirt. I'm talking real Versace, not the junk they sold at Diamond's in Shaker Heights, although all of us stopped through Diamond's from time to time. Wearing the real, and keeping it real, separated you from the rest of the pack.

Everybody knew my name at the Millennium, a downtown nightclub that young people from all over the city went to on Sunday nights. I skipped the line at the Cotton Club, a grimy basement on 131st and Miles that was supposed to be for teens but had grown folks all up in it, twenty-two-year-old dudes dating girls who were sixteen. I posted up in the Uptown Grill with older hustlers who drank their cognac neat. Once in a while I snuck into Club Togo. I was eighteen years old with a face that looked thirteen, hanging with guys who were forty. Like, really hanging with them—spending, gambling, and hustling on their level. If a gambler from out of town wanted to get it on, best believe he heard my name, and I got word of his. The Kid was in the know.

Cleveland was a big city, of course, but a shrinking one. Compared to places like New York or Chicago, we had more hustlers competing for the same pot of money and territory. You had to be on top of your game to get money in Cleveland with so many other sharks swimming in the same water. On the legal side of things, bigger cities had more opportunity in terms of music, fashion, and the creative industries that Black people had historically gravitated to as we were shut out of the mainstream. If I'd grown up in Atlanta or Los Angeles, I could have gone to a fashion school, or stood outside a record label until I charmed my way into an internship. None of that was available in Cleveland. By senior year in high school, it was clear that I needed to find the right stage.

Senior Night for the basketball team arrived. Dad was there and Peaches was not, as usual. I had resigned myself to her absence by this point. If people ever asked me where she was, I told them straight-up, "My mother's not here because she's dealing with substance abuse." I still wished she could have seen me start my last home game, but I kept those feelings hidden, even from myself.

My family dealt with so much in real life, supporting me at a basketball game wasn't at the top of their list of priorities. My sister Brandie was going through things with her own children by that time. Meco was going hard in the streets and came to a game or two. I had friends from around the way who might watch me sometimes, but how far can you expect people to travel if you're not playing major minutes? I got accustomed to my people not being there, because I understood the real world. I didn't take offense because I knew the game that was really being played. In the dope game, you gotta hug that block. You got to bend them corners, you got to be giant on that spot. That's where my brother and all my friends were at—everybody but me, a five-foot-seven and three-quarters shooting guard playing in his last regular-season high school basketball game. Dad wore a three-piece brown suit. The creases in his pants were sharp enough to cut bread.

We ended up losing in the state championship game to Philo that year. After winning the title the previous two seasons, we thought Philo would be easy. We underestimated them and stayed up partying and gambling the night before. They held the ball and slowed down the game, there was no shot clock, and they beat us.

My life as an athlete was over.

When the end of the school year approached, I decided to attend the University of Akron. I knew how much Dad valued education, and how proud he would be if I went to college. I liked school, it was interesting, plus different from what most guys from my neighborhood were into. At the same time, the streets were still calling me. The shoeboxes in my tiny bedroom at my grandma's house held well into the five figures, sometimes six after a big dice game. My weed business had reached a point where I almost turned down more business than I took. I had one foot in the streets, the other in school. That had worked for me through four years of high school, so I figured I would keep it going in college. I didn't want to go to school too far away, because I had so much business jumping off in Cleveland. Akron was only a forty-minute drive, and I figured that was a happy medium. I would have to do it smarter, though. I knew I could gain access to a new clientele in Akron, but I would have to carry weed in my car along Route 8 and Interstate 77, which was a high risk. I had a lot of thinking to do, a lot of decisions to make.

I felt prepared for this next stage of my life. I handled all the Akron enrollment and tuition myself. I wasn't on scholarship and paid the couple thousand dollars. The summer of 1999, before I left for college, was like any other summer for me. Summer was about getting to it. Up early every day, at the park gambling, taking care of my product, stunting at block parties, clubs, out and about doing this, that, and the third. Summer was also about trying to stay alive, although I had internalized my environment to the point where I didn't know that's what I was doing. Niggas die in the summer. They die year-round, but the summer was more dangerous because more people were outside, acting wild and free and wanting to try certain things. Jay-Z had a song at that time, "Come and Get Me," that really resonated with me: *Yo, your summer's 'bout to get hot / Niggas home from jail and they plottin'.* Summer was a time to press my bet, but with intention and precision.

Once I got a letter telling me the date and address for college orientation, I figured out the directions and showed up by myself. August came and I arrived at campus for the start of classes driving a Cutlass with gold Daytons, a bit more flashy than usual, enough to let people know that I was not your average freshman. I had a dorm room, although I only slept there one or two nights per week. I signed up for business courses and was engaged with the material. Sometimes I got a page on campus from somebody back home, and I hopped in my car and met them in forty minutes. By the end of September, I had settled nicely into college life. I started to wonder what my next move might be.

Then I got a call from my sister Brandie.

"Dad is sick," she said. "They think it's cancer."

RULE

**Your Worst Experience Can Be Your Best Credential.**

## 19

## LOST IN THE GAME

knew it was bad when his hair started falling out. Then his eyebrows and toenails went. I watched his body deteriorate as the cancer spread from his bladder. Not in my worst nightmares did I see this coming. Dad was only fifty-three years old.

I transferred from Akron to Cleveland State University to be closer to him. Every morning I got up early and visited Dad before class, first in the hospital and then, during his hospice care, at the house on Ardenall Avenue, where he lived with his wife and my sister Nicki. I was staying with Meco's girlfriend while Meco was in jail, and one night I couldn't get into the house. I was locked out with no key, maybe because she was tired of me being around or didn't want me in her business. I was too grown to still live with my grandma, so I decided it was time to get my first crib, in Richmond Heights, apartment 304 in the Dorchester Village complex. My little one-bedroom rental had wall-to-wall carpet, which I thought was top shelf. I went out and bought all new furniture, plus a 61-inch Hitachi television from B&B Appliance. I carried my double life from high school to Akron and then right back to Cleveland State. I kept my hustling private, slow and low. My gambling didn't change, because it took my mind off my dad's illness, and because it was my job—dice provided more than half of my income at that time.

One night I went back to Grandma Johnnie Mae's house and was just sitting there, worrying about Dad. She encouraged me to get busy with something to take my mind off things. My friends also wanted to get me out the house, because word was spreading that Dad's condition was serious. Duck paged me and said I should roll with him to see Black Rob perform at the Millennium. Rob was blazing hot at the time with his hit song "Whoa!" My grandmother said, "If anything happens, I'll page you 9-1-1."

I'm at the Millennium and Black Rob is on stage. He hadn't got to "Whoa" yet when I felt my pager vibrate, and of course it said "9-1-1." Duck drove me to Dad's house. Soon after, our pastor arrived, the Reverend Larry Howard from Greater Friendship Baptist Church, and we prayed over Dad. I was standing next to his bedside when he left this world on February 28, 2000.

I was nineteen years old. As much as I thought I was prepared for him to die, I still cried like a baby that night.

The time between Dad's death and his burial was a blur. Two thousand people showed up for the funeral at Greater Friendship. That's when the full impact and magnitude of his life hit me. Two thousand people, not for a politician or an athlete, but for a corner store owner who tried to help everyone he could. I rode to the funeral in a limo with Grandma Johnnie Mae; my dad's wife, Justine; and Nicki. Meco was still locked up and couldn't come. My mom showed up. She and Brandie sat across the aisle from me and Justine. I don't think Mom ever got over Dad's death—over having such a great man in her life, but never taking advantage of what he could have given her. Just knowing that she repeatedly messed up something good because she was strung out on that dope.

Sitting with thousands of people in that church, looking at Dad's body in his coffin, I felt more alone than I ever had in my life.

My backbone was gone, my support system, the man who would always give me his last. I began thinking about something I thought I had put away for good.

I wrestled with that thought for ten days after the funeral, trying to avoid something that had been stalking me since my earliest days on the block. I examined the idea from every angle, considered what it would mean to reject or embrace it. I thought about every strategy and avenue.

On the tenth day after the funeral, I was sitting behind the counter at the store, in the chair Dad would never sit in again.

Mom and Brandie were back in St. Louis. Meco was behind bars. My mourning period was over. It was time to do for self.

I walked over to the pay phone and made a call. Later that day, the man I called met me in the parking lot of a nearby grocery store, and he sold me a large quantity of cocaine.

. . .

I felt like I needed to press, strap up my boots, be more of a man. When Dad was alive there were some things I just wouldn't do, and at the top of that list was selling coke. Dad had been the only thing standing between me and full immersion in the streets. That was the line he drew my freshman year in high school, when he said he'd take me out of this world if I didn't focus on my education.

After he died, everything changed.

I put all his warnings out of my head. Without the moral compass of my dad, I got lost in the competitive nature of the dope game. It was basically inevitable that I would take that next step, given everything I had done up to that point, the person I had become. My guys and I always told each other, "If you're gonna ball, ball all the way out." Finally, that's what I was doing.

I took those ten days to figure out my entry point. I couldn't call just anybody for the product. Selling hard drugs was something that I never really wanted to do. I still wasn't feeling great about it. But after they put Dad in the ground, I figured out who to buy from, I made the call, and the transaction took place—the first of many.

It would be easy to say I decided to sell drugs because I saw it happening all around me, but that's just partially true. I can't say that I was strictly a product of my environment.

Yeah, I gambled and hustled because I was raised by and around people who did those things. If I had been born in a neighborhood that wasn't filled with drugs and violence, in a city where government policies hadn't created and maintained a ghetto for Black people, my path would have been much different. But my environment doesn't explain why I crushed dice games in elementary school, or built a clientele so loyal they waited all day to cop weed from me after class. Living in the ghetto doesn't explain why I could move safely among killers on hostile blocks.

I did those things because I was driven by the competition and the challenge of it.

The hunger to reach for the highest, the most, the best had grown in me—or maybe it's something I was born with. I pursued success in this new game using skills that I was taught, first by my dad and then by my environment: numbers, relationships, entrepreneurship, empathy, strategy. Those skills were polished and sharpened in the streets, they are what made me successful, and every success fueled my hunger for more.

I don't want to dodge responsibility for my actions by saying "the hood made me do it." That's just part of my story. Where I'm from, a lot of people aspired to be major in the dope game, but very few made it happen. The desire to compete, my entrepre-neurial drive and mind for business, the refusal to be complacent, the need to chase better things than what was right in front of me—that was the challenge that excited me.

That's what drove me then, and what drives me now. It's not just a drive to succeed in the game as it currently exists, but a desire to try and change the game, to create opportunities for people who have been locked out of access to power, people like me back then, trying to find a way. I couldn't change the game in the streets. It just wasn't possible, because that's the only game played with no refs and no written rules. My business today has refs and rules, but no integrity or honor, and definitely none of the consequences that I grew up with. I understood the rules of engagement when I was selling drugs, and I understand them now. Only now, I can refuse to abide by those rules. The agent playbook says the more creden-tials you have, the better position you're in. I knew how much dis-respect there was among agents and executives in the NBA for someone with my background, but I saw a huge opportunity in the fact that nobody else had my experiences. Experiences are just as important as credentials and whatever money you might have been born into. My experiences placed me in a great position to help others. This is what they don't teach in the traditional institutions, whether that's college or sports agencies—that academic training means nothing if you can't use it to distinguish yourself from your competition. I came to the NBA offering something totally differ-ent than my peers did. This is why those of us who can beat the odds and overcome negative environments have an unbelievable head start, if we can only realize the gifts that our struggles have given us. This is why I'm so lucky.

Today, my experiences are an asset. But first, they almost killed me.

# PART IV

# MY
# DEMONS

RULE

**Hang On Until You're Dealt
a Winning Hand.**

## 20

# THE SOUL WAS GONE

had been friends with Duck since we met at the Cotton Club in middle school. We shared an appreciation for fashion, gambling, and the desire to do things differently, and we also came from families with a similar conflicting mix of strong moral guidance and absolute dysfunction. Duck jumped off the porch into selling crack when he was fourteen, but I had held out. Now that I was all in, we cliqued up and moved as a unit.

Relationships were always one of my strengths, and in the dope game, who you know is of paramount importance. That "plug" will make or break you. Not long after Dad died, I organically came across a great situation that elevated my start-up operation with Duck. All of a sudden, we were on an entirely new level.

I left Cleveland State and took a couple of business courses at

Bryant & Stratton for another year, but with everything I had going on, I couldn't do the college thing. Knowing what I know now, I would have stayed and taken more classes in arts and sciences or African American studies. Not because I need them for my work as an agent, but because I wish I'd had a chance to spend some time learning for the sake of learning.

That said, my street education was about to hit PhD-level.

We moved weight, stacked paper, and did what teenagers with money do: bought clothes, partied at Vel's on Thursdays, the Spy Bar on Fridays, and the Millennium on Sundays. We chased girls and bought more clothes. We started traveling to Philly, New York, and other cities, popping up at big concerts and NBA All-Star Games. At home, we became hood royalty, skipping the line at nightclubs and sitting at the best tables in restaurants. When it came to clothes, I was on my peacock vibe. This was the peak of the baggy-clothes era, but soon we went against that grain and slimmed down our style early, to the point where ignorant dudes said our fitted clothes looked gay. Like Wall Street traders who moved the stock market based on what they bought and sold, we dictated the culture in Cleveland and set trends instead of following them. I also fell head over heels in love with jewelry. I had always liked necklaces, but now I could really get creative. I copped platinum Rolexes, Jacob chains, a platinum *R* pendant, and a platinum-and-diamond pinky ring with my initials, like my dad used to wear.

I bought my first house at age nineteen, a place on Hinsdale

Road for a hundred and three thousand dollars. I got a mortgage with Fifth Third Bank, listed my occupation as "entrepreneur," and strategized about how to invest in more real estate. We started a company called Put It On Entertainment to throw our own parties, and I got more interested in making music. Like a lot of hustlers, I had lyrics in my head about my experiences and what I was going through. I recorded songs under the name Revenue Rich, and executive produced songs by other artists.

By dabbling in all kinds of financial and creative endeavors, I was beginning to understand how to harness culture. I understood what was cool and why trends caught on. So much of it was rooted in Black culture—what we listen to, the way we talk, what we wear, how we communicate. This drives the popularity of so many industries, including professional sports. Back then I never thought I would be able to work at Nike, but meanwhile I was spending the equivalent of a Nike employee's salary on my purchases. Now that I know how a sneaker company's infrastructure works, I can pair that knowledge with my experience as an avid self-taught consumer to really drive value. But I was all over the place back then, trying out different ideas and methods of expressing my creativity and business sense. The consistent theme was to not be constrained by how everyone else did things. We dressed differently and ate at places other guys didn't know about. We researched what we bought and educated ourselves about what things had real value. And all the time, in the absence of my father, I was trying to understand what it meant to be a man. Even when it came to hustling,

our crew had our own way of going about it, operating by principles other guys didn't care about.

In a game with no rules, we had to make our own.

. . .

I dated my childhood girlfriend Candace on and off over the years.
After I got my first place, Candace moved in, and we started trying
to create a life together. I was too old to keep living with my grandmother, but too young to realize what it meant to live with a partner. I thought that as long as I took care of Candace, like my dad
took care of my mom, I was fulfilling my responsibilities. I didn't
understand all the other work involved in a relationship. Given that
neither of us had ever lived around an intact family, we didn't have
a solid idea of what healthy relationships looked like. I loved my
father and he loved me dearly. But I never lived in his home.

Don't get me wrong, I'm not angry at Dad for that. Staying
with him full-time wasn't a real option given he was married to a
woman who was not my mother. Me never living under his roof
elevates his commitment in my mind, because he had to make an
effort to have a relationship with me. That effort shows how much
he cared. My dad had to go the extra mile to take care of me and
understand who I was.

There's been a change in the NBA in the last ten years or so,
with more kids coming from two-parent families and stable homes.
Older guys in the league are more likely to come from the type of

environment I grew up in—we're children of the crack era. That era ended in the early 2000s, when the suicidal nature of crack finally gave it a stigma that moved our community away from it. Most of this new NBA generation has both parents present, no matter what income bracket they come from, which is a wonderful thing. But they also lack some of the qualities that we developed out of necessity. We traveled a much tougher road. I think my younger clients see that experience in me, and they know that I have something special to offer them because of it.

I never got any fairy tales from my father. He didn't prepare me to be a loving, compassionate partner in an intimate relationship. He prepared me for war. Because that's what was outside the door. A fucking war. Mostly fought by traumatized child soldiers who never even learned what the war was about, but also had no idea how to end it. To this day, whether I'm driving through Beverly Hills or Cleveland, when the police get behind me, I start calculating what decision to make if those lights start flashing, even though I know I'm clean. That's what trauma does to you.

Candace and I were two traumatized kids, playing house. I wasn't trying to be in love with anybody. I didn't love nothing but the game.

. . .

Our family kept R&J Confectionary open, and I still went over there to work the register and help Uncle Joe. About a month after my dad died, I was at the store watching the local news on the little TV behind the counter. The sports segment came on with the results of the high school state championship basketball game. This tiny point guard named Dru Joyce III, from St. Vincent–St. Mary in Akron, went crazy from the three-point line. He shot seven-for-seven and St. Vincent–St. Mary won the title. A freshman named LeBron James led all scorers with twenty-five points.

*That's a cool little team,* I thought.

We tried to keep the store going, but the soul was gone. Without Dad, everything fell apart. It closed a couple years after he died. One of my biggest regrets in life is not buying that building, because the most important address in my life is now an empty lot.

. . .

Diddy was the biggest force in hip-hop at this time, when his name was still Puff Daddy. Jay-Z's music was superior to everything else, but Jay hadn't hit his mogul phase yet. Diddy was that dude. I was inspired by how he used music, fashion, personality, and taste to create revenue and a brand. Very few athletes seemed cool to me, because the stars were older and disconnected from what young people were living. Michael Jordan was still the dominant player, but he cultivated a mainstream, suit-and-tie image. I loved Jordan on the court, but there was no organic connection on a cultural level between his world and mine. Little did we know that the sports world was on the cusp of a huge cultural change. Athletes

from my generation were about to take over from the old heads—
and our generation was culturally inspired by the Diddys, Jay-Zs,
and Allen Iversons way more than Jordan. I don't want to down-
play MJ's influence on us in terms of business, and how he lever-
aged his athletic talent into tremendous wealth. But a lot of what
makes athletes popular is style and aesthetics. Jordan came into the
league and led a major aesthetic shift: bald head, bigger shorts,
and, of course, his signature sneakers. But a new style was emerg-
ing all over the country, led by a younger hip-hop generation of
moguls, hustlers, ballplayers, and performers. In Cleveland, that
style and aesthetic belonged to me and my crew.

We were able to watch that culture being born all over the
country. We stacked money all year—*stack, stack, stack, stack,
stack*—then hit the road: Cincinnati for the jazz festival; Philly, DC,
or Atlanta for the NBA All-Star Game. Today, when I go to All-Star
Weekend I might have as many as seven clients in the game. Being
on the inside of the festivities is rewarding, but I probably had
more fun when I was younger, showing up just to shop and stunt.
Women came looking to bag a player or a hustler, and we were
looking for them. On K Street in DC, I might see some girls in the
next car over and hop out of mine. You had to strike a certain posture leaning into the window of their car, then leaning back to look
around, make sure you're showing your watch. It was a thing. In
Philly we stayed at the Hyatt on Broad Street. I would pull up to
Club Egypt on Spring Garden, driving the S-Type Jag on Giovan-
nas. To pay the valet, I'd pull twenty thousand dollars out of my

pocket, peel off a couple bills, and say, "Here's two hundred to keep my car up front." It was a real thing. Now I'm standing on line, asking this and that pretty woman if they want to come in with us. We got fifteen people at five hundred a head, I'm counting the bills out my bankroll, *whap whap whap*—it made me feel a certain way to be seen with that money in my hand. It gave me that same high I'd been chasing since I was a kid in Jordan 4s, but without doing drugs.

My mom *did* do drugs, though. And her constant struggle and deterioration embodied the harm I was causing with the poison I was now selling to fund my lifestyle. It was always so close, the luxury and the pain. This is what I still struggle with—the moral cost of my come up and the disappointment my father would have felt if he could've seen me in those days. I never felt good about selling drugs, but I compartmentalized that feeling from my pursuit of the money. It hurts to admit this, but when I was stunting at those All-Star Games, I didn't even think about my mother. That's how resigned I was to her condition, and how consumed I was by trying to win the only game I thought I would be allowed to play. I told myself that selling drugs was doing what I had to do to survive, even though blowing through thousands of dollars was about indulgence, not survival. Even now, when I've long since accepted responsibility for my enormous mistakes, I'm sometimes uncertain about just how much guilt I should feel when pharmaceutical companies get away with addicting millions of people to opioids. Big Pharma—wealthy, fully grown men and women in enormous corporations—made a lot more money than any teenage drug dealer in my neighborhood. Then again, the inescapable fact is that I was inflicting damage to *my neighborhood*. After my dad died, sometimes I would suddenly be struck by a feeling: *Wow, what am I even doing? This ain't me*. But that feeling never hit when I was gripping twenty thousand at Club Egypt. It came when I tried to imagine an endgame, and started to think that the whole scenario was a trap for people like me, people who came from the bottom. When I sat in the fifth row of Philips Arena in Atlanta for Michael Jordan's last All-Star Game, I could have been sitting there as a senior at Morehouse College, with a mom who was a doctor or a lawyer. But Peaches didn't take that route. It's not even her fault. The deck of life was stacked against us. I played the hands I was dealt. Most guys from my background only get to play one hand. But some of us are lucky, make it through a couple of hands, and then get a chance to deal. When you deal, you get to shuffle the deck. My goal in life was to find a way to stay at the table long enough to get my turn to shuffle the deck and deal myself a winning hand. My goal was to keep playing, like Kenny Rogers sang, until the dealing's done.

In the meantime, all I could do is play the cards in my hand. That, and learn to live with regrets.

RULE

**Be a Star in Your Role.**

## 21

## OUT THE TRUNK

liked to buy sneakers and put them on ice for months, just waiting for the perfect occasion and outfit. I had some black Bo Jacksons in the stash and wanted to pair them with a Latrell Sprewell Knicks jersey. You might wonder how those two things go together, but I didn't like to coordinate colors that looked too matchy-matchy. I was more into complementary accents. I wanted the white Sprewell jersey because his number "8" was outlined in black and there were black accents down the side, which would pop when paired with the black sneakers. I would never wear the white, orange, and blue Bo Jacksons with the white, orange, and blue Knicks jersey. Anybody could do that.

Early in 2001, my friend Mike E and I went on a shopping trip to New York City, and of course we hit the NBA Store on Fifth

Avenue in midtown. I found my Sprewell and was standing in the checkout line when some unfamiliar jerseys caught my eye. I got out of line to go look. I knew the players and teams, but I hadn't seen the uniform styles before because they were from the 1960s and '70s. I saw a Bill Russell jersey from the Boston Celtics, an Elgin Baylor from the Los Angeles Lakers, and an Oscar Robertson from when he played for the Milwaukee Bucks. The name HARD-WOOD CLASSICS was on the labels.

I loved the feel and detail and thought the jerseys were dope, so I bought the Baylor and the Robertson for almost four hundred dollars apiece. I liked Russell's Celtics jersey, but it felt a little too plain for me. I knew exactly what I was going to do with the others. I had a pair of Timberlands in mind to go with the Oscar Robert-son. I wore the Elgin Baylor under a navy blue Polo leather coat that I bought from the Polo store in Philadelphia.

Back home, when I wore those jerseys to the club, the response was off the chain. Everybody kept saying, "Where'd you get that? I need me one of those!" This is before you could easily buy clothes on the internet, and you had to show up to a real-life store to buy anything. I had always been known around the city for fashion and having unique items, but these new throwbacks took my name to an even higher level.

I had a little makeshift office in my house with a computer. I went online, typed in a search for "Hardwood Classics," and a store in Atlanta called Distant Replays popped up. I called the store and the owner, Andy Hyman, answered the phone.

I talked to Andy about what jerseys he had in stock and got excited when he mentioned all the football and baseball joints that were not on his website: Tony Gwynn with the Padres, Pete Rose with the Reds, Randall Cunningham with the Eagles, even some names I had never heard of despite considering myself a sports historian from watching all those games as a kid. I bought three jerseys during that first phone call, for about a thousand dollars total, including overnight shipping. I spent another thousand dollars the next week, and another thousand the week after that. I did that for about eight weeks straight. Everybody in Cleveland was Polo'd out, so when I started showing up in Jim Browns and Hank Aarons, it caused a major sensation. I wore each jersey once—they were one and done—and then stacked them in my closet.

After about two months of this, I called Andy and said, "I'd like to invest in your business."

"Really?" he said. "If you're serious, come on down to Atlanta and we'll talk."

When I said I wanted to invest in his business, I didn't really know what I had in mind. I knew I had money, though. And I knew I could sell water to a well.

My friend D Hodge went to Cleveland Heights High School, and a bunch of his friends went to college at Morehouse and Clark in Atlanta. When I told Hodge I wanted to go down to Atlanta, he said he had a homeboy with an apartment in Marietta, we could crash there while I did my thing. We flew down and I slept on Hodge's friend's couch. The next morning I woke up and went to meet Andy at noon, at an Irish pub next to his store on East Paces Ferry Road in Buckhead.

Andy was a cool dude, a middle-aged white entrepreneur who started Distant Replays in a kiosk at the Greenbriar Mall. Andy is the one who sold OutKast their jerseys when they wore the rainbow Astros and the Falcons' Steve Bartkowski in videos and photo shoots. We talked and Andy told me that he couldn't let me invest, but if I worked in his store one weekend each month, he'd give me 40 percent off all my purchases. I agreed and shook hands before he could change his mind. Andy could have offered me 10 percent off and it would have been a good deal for me. I was trying to figure this whole jersey thing out. I was trying to figure out my life.

I started flying down to Atlanta once a month like we agreed, staying at a Marriott Residence Inn up the street from Distant Replays. I'd been working in my dad's store my whole life, so working for Andy was a layup. I ran the credit card machine, worked the register, and dealt with customers on the floor. The store sold all kinds of sports apparel in addition to jerseys—this was the South, before hip-hop fashion went fully mainstream, so you might have a white father and son who didn't look cool in jerseys but wanted T-shirts and hats. Andy showed me how much of a market there was for all this other sports stuff. And at the end of each weekend, I had the pick of the litter with jerseys. They cost three hundred in the store; Andy sold them to me for one-sixty.

I flew home each Sunday with around twenty to thirty jerseys and sold them for the price on the tag: three hundred, sometimes four hundred or four-fifty. They moved right out the trunk of my Toyota Camry. I had no overhead, and my price point was firm. I knew the value of my product.

Man, those jerseys sold better than crack. A big part of their value came from the fact that I was the one selling them. My reputation connected to the product made it fly. People said, "Why should I go to the mall, and maybe pay a higher price, when I can get it from Rich?" Plus I advised people on what to buy; they didn't even need to like the player whose name was on the back. I put a lot of my old sports knowledge to use, bringing back facts from all those late-night games I watched alone as a kid or on the floor of Grandma Johnnie Mae's house. I also explained to customers how the authentic jerseys with sewn-on letters and numbers were of much higher quality, durability, and historical significance than the replica jerseys with iron-on letters and numbers. I'd pull up to the park or the dice game and *boom*—five jerseys would sell just like that. I met the Cleveland Browns fullback Corey Fuller at a dice game, and when he saw what I was wearing he told me to pull up to his house out in Westlake. He bought two or three jerseys. CC Sabathia, in his early years with the Indians, bought some. I had all those guys. It got to the point where word got out that I'd be in a random parking lot and the customers would come right to me. Moving jerseys out of the trunk of my car wasn't nearly as dangerous as moving drugs and it didn't tug at my conscience. It made me feel free.

I never would have had access to the jerseys if I hadn't been willing to put my ego aside and commit to being a role player with Andy, unpacking boxes and working the sales floor. Andy telling me he wouldn't make me a partner in his business was like my grandmother saying she wouldn't give me a key to her house. It was a humbling challenge, and I was fine with it. "Out the trunk" is a mentality that still fuels me to this day, and it comes from more than just selling jerseys. It's about chasing down every little opportunity, putting in extra effort, and doing whatever it takes to improve your position. Phil Knight started out the trunk with Nike, carrying boxes of sneakers and racks of clothes around. "Out the trunk" forces you to interact with people, to develop communication skills, to understand the value of time. All my hustles brought me into direct contact with people—I call that kind of personal touch in business hand-to-hand combat. There's something special in hand-to-hand combat that teaches you a whole set of skills you can't quantify on a test. I learned much more coming up out the trunk than if I'd been born with a billionaire grandfather.

. . .

Andy was amazed by the volume I was moving, so he asked to come up to Cleveland and see for himself. The day before he arrived, I went to every block and told my people, "If you see me roll up with a white dude, he's not the police, he's my business partner—just buy whatever I got." We drove all over the hood, jerseys flying out the trunk, and Andy was blown away. After that, I was buying so much product, Andy had to put me on to his connect—Peter Capolino, who founded Mitchell & Ness in Philadelphia. That was the company that had the NBA license, manufactured the jerseys, and sold them to Andy.

Just like in the dope game, I had organically come across a great situation that elevated my operation. I had the plug.

I made nice money with the whole jersey experience, ten or fifteen thousand a month when it was really popping. More importantly, it offered a glimpse of a new way of life. It helped me see a future where I could move into legitimate businesses, and away from selling drugs. Because the streets were starting to weigh on my mind.

RULE

**Have Faith—You're Built for More than You Can See.**

# 22

## LOOKING FOR AN OUT

An OG named Noah ran one of the biggest gambling spots in Cleveland inside a Sunoco gas station on Superior. All the heavyweight gamblers went there, pro athletes, big-time dope dealers, and Black business owners with ties to the underworld community.

Let me say something about the concept of the underworld: It's very real, in an almost literal sense. My everyday activities took place in a world that most people never see. You and I might both be having a breakfast sandwich in a restaurant, but I'm there for a reason that has nothing to do with food. As you're eating, all you see is a young man enjoying his sandwich. You may notice that on the other side of the diner is another guy eating a sandwich. You may or may not notice that moments after I get up and go to the bathroom, he gets up and goes to the bathroom. You definitely don't see that in that bathroom, a transaction takes place. Both of us come out, finish our sandwiches, and leave. That's the underworld, invisible and right in front of your face.

Multiple realities coexist. You just need the right lens to see them. When I go to NBA games, people always ask me why I don't cheer and yell and get all riled up like a fan. I tell them, "Because I'm watching a different game." That means I'm paying attention to the subtle and even unseen variables—how the players relate to each other, which players seem distracted or tired, which players are pressing because of trade rumors or a new contract, which players have checked out for personal or professional reasons, who is frustrated, who is in the zone. All of that is what drives the final score.

Duck and I pulled up to this Sunoco in Duck's mom's Mitsubishi Montero. We had an older guy with us who went by the name of Ums, because when he talked he couldn't stop saying "Umm, ummm . . ." Ums was the type of dude who never shot the dice himself, but would borrow fifty or a hundred dollars at the game and bet the dice going out. He'd bet on what I was rolling. We called that "riding the horse."

The process of getting access to the game was to go inside the Sunoco, walk to the cash register, and give the cashier whatever the code was, like "Is Freddie here?" Then you walk past the back cooler and a buzzer goes off. The buzzer opens a door at the back of the store. It looks like the door to a custodian's room, but it opens into a short hallway, and on the other side of that hallway is a door that opens into a full-blown gambling parlor. The room is soundproof, with a carpet for the dice and cameras everywhere. It's a small room that could fit about ten or fifteen people comfortably, but sometimes there would be more like fifty people jammed up in there.

This particular day, Duck, Ums, and I walked in and the spot was on tilt. It seemed like everybody in Cleveland with money was there. I had about five thousand cash in my pocket. The Sunoco station was situated in the middle of the city, so you had guys from down the projects, from Up the Way, from all kinds of different neighborhoods. Noah's was known as a gentleman's game, but sometimes guys who didn't like each other were there. Me and Duck were strapped, for sure.

By this time, Cleveland had moved from craps to three dice, or what they call cee-lo on the East Coast. Three dice had taken over the whole gambling scene, which made it harder for me to roll the numbers I wanted, because it added another variable to deal with. At Noah's we also had to roll the dice up against a wall, which made it tougher for slicksters like me to influence the outcome. If the roll didn't bounce off the wall, it didn't count. Noah's game was more about pure luck than skill. I had to be there, though. Gambling for the hustler is like golfing for the rich man. The dice house was our country club, where we went to enjoy ourselves while strengthening relationships and maintaining visibility among colleagues. And if you think they don't gamble on golf at the country club, you're crazy.

The other guys at Noah's started running through my bank. My first five thousand is gone, I gotta go back out to Duck's car and get more money. We had a bunch of money and some other things in the trunk of his ride. The game was like Jay-Z described in "Where I'm From": *It always starts out with three dice and "shoot the five" / Niggas thought they deuce was live then I hit 'em with trips / And I reached down for they money, pa, forget about this . . .*

That's exactly how we were thinking. Only in this game, I was the one losing. I kept going back to the trunk again and again.

Usually I was good about knowing when to quit, but today was different because I was getting ready to re-up. That's what the cash in the trunk was for. I never should have risked that money, but now I couldn't lose it because then I wouldn't be able to buy my product. I had to win my money back.

At this point it's safe to say that I'm addicted to gambling. A functional addict, with some measure of control, but an addict for sure. The difference between a degenerate gambler and a hustler with a functional gambling addiction is control. If I was on my grind and needed to focus on product rather than dice, or if I took a major gambling loss and needed to rebuild my bank, I'd tell myself, "I'm not gambling for thirty days," and I wouldn't gamble for thirty days. I knew people who didn't have that kind of control. But that day in Noah's spot, I came as close as I ever did to losing control. I was down twenty-five thousand dollars—more money than I've ever lost in my life. Ain't no more in the trunk. The dice are in my hand. We're shooting for five thousand dollars a throw, which is all I have left in my pocket.

The dice whispered, *Let Duck roll.*

Once again, I could hear the dice talk.

*You ice-cold.*

*Let Duck roll.*

I hand the dice to Duck and say, "Go get it."

Duck rolls three deuces—we win. Now our bank is ten thousand. Instead of cutting the bank and pocketing some of it, we let that ten thousand lay. That allowed more people to bet. Duck rolls again, wins again. We go on a run, throwing "big sixes," which are combinations—one-one-six, two-two-six, all the way up to six-six-six—that win points. We come all the way back to break even and decide it's time to be out.

I can't lie, coming so close to that large of a loss was a new feeling. A mixture of shame that I let myself get so deep in the hole, and fear about what would have happened if I lost it all. As we walked to the car, Ums was laughing to himself. Me and Duck looked at him like, *What you on?*

Ums said, "Man, if I knew y'all had that much money in your car, I would have robbed both of you myself!"

We still laugh about that to this day. But the thing is, Ums might not have been joking.

And what if Duck hadn't rolled that big six when we were down to our last? What if I had lost control of myself and let my addiction take me under? What could have happened next?

. . .

Not too long after, I got a taste of what bad luck felt like. I got snaked by some people I shouldn't have been dealing with and took a huge loss:

A quarter million.

In cash.

They got my watch, too, which brought my total loss to about three hundred thousand. I was moving too fast, trying to make things shake, and went against some of my normal precautions. It was a major blow, almost crippling, but I had to put it behind me and keep on pushing. My brother, Meco, was home from a fourteen-month jail bid by this time, and he was way, way more upset than I was. I told him to move on, but Meco was ready to take matters into his own hands.

I'm actually thankful we never found the guys who snaked us, because we would have had to kill them. And then what? I still think about that all the time. Even if I wasn't there when they got dealt with, I would have had to live with that. Two dudes come up dead, I know what it was. I don't need that in my life. That's not how you get your blessings.

It may seem strange to say this about dope dealing, but I had principles when I was out there. I had integrity. I had respect for people, even on their worst day. A lot of times I was in position to come at people to the point where I could have had somebody do whatever I wanted them to do. I thank God every day that I didn't go that route. Those demons, I didn't want no part of them.

I had different demons: In the back of my mind, I knew that my mom was somewhere out there, using what I was selling. I knew the look my dad would have had on his face when he found out I was selling poison.

The financial losses were bad, but those demons made me start looking for a way to change my situation. I eased up on moving product, bought another house, and tried to make some real money with music—typical dope-boy moves. But at the same time, if I ever needed a quick ten thousand, I got in the kitchen and made it happen.

The rapper Scarface dropped a song about this time that really grabbed me: "Someday," with Faith Evans on the hook and produced by the Neptunes:

*Who am I to judge a man when I'm a man myself / In the dark, trying to get me some help . . .*

I kept that song on repeat as I drove around the city, looking for a way out.

. . .

One of the places Duck and I liked to eat was a diner called the Cleveland Deli. They had great chicken wings. It was on St. Clair heading toward downtown, outside of our hood, a noteworthy place among regular citizens in the city. There was a time when we went there every day, on our lunch break from hustling.

As we were walking out of the diner one day, an older Black man came up on us from what seemed like out of nowhere. He was wearing a trench coat over a suit and a classy fedora-style hat. I don't know how else to say this: He looked like a gentleman.

"Young man," the gentleman told me, "your life is about to change for the better."

I was confused. Who was this guy, and what was he talking about? I started to ask his name but he spoke again:

"Some things are going to break your way," he said.

Duck and I looked at each other, trying to figure out what was going on. When we looked back toward the gentleman, he was gone. Like, he was nowhere to be seen, and it happened too quickly for him to walk away and turn a corner. He came out of nowhere and he disappeared to nowhere.

The whole thing was really, really strange. Duck called it a supernatural event. Then we took our bags of chicken wings and went back to selling dope.

. . .

My man Wink hosted dice games in the basement of his house on 105th and St. Clair, off Empire. I was there one night when *BANG!*—a huge crash came from the front room. Police smashed in the door with a battering ram. The cops had their guns out and shouted for everybody to get down on the floor. They handcuffed us and searched the spot. Apparently they had bad information because there were no drugs in the house, and it's not illegal for friends to gamble among themselves.

I had one problem, though. A big one. My car was parked outside, dirty as shit.

They had a bunch of us handcuffed on the curb outside Wink's house. I could see my Camry parked a couple driveways down.

The K9 unit pulled up.

Out came the drug-sniffing dog.

It got to my ride and started sniffing, sniffing, sniffing . . .

. . . and then moved on to the next car.

The cops eventually let everybody go and I slept in my own bed that night, but I was shook down to my bones. After my gambling addiction got me down twenty-five thousand dollars, after getting snaked for two hundred and fifty thousand, and now this—the total effect made me think harder than I ever had about what I was doing. It made me want to bury the demons that crawled into my conscience when I thought about selling what my mother was using. It made me see something new on my father's face—not disappointment, but disgust.

I had been toeing the line of being in or out of the game. I was like a wide receiver making a catch on the sideline, with his toes inbounds and the rest of his body out. In my mind I'm out of the game, but at certain moments I'm still in it, tying up loose ends and bringing a few moves to completion. And in that world, you can't tie up loose ends unless you're still in it. You can think you're out all you want, but you ain't.

I had made it to the highest level of the game in my city. My name was known throughout Cleveland, and beyond. But that came with a whole lot of paranoid nights and days. I could barely trust anyone. Police only needed to have one good day to lock me up, while I needed to have three hundred and sixty-five great days to remain free.

That close call at Wink's put a lot of things in perspective. That's when I knew God had a plan for me, because the door to my car was unlocked. If they open that door, I'm going to the federal penitentiary. I don't know for how long, but I'm going because I got money, I got product, and I got a pistol. Those things together make it a federal case.

For that door to be open and that dog to be right there and not bark—how many illegal searches have there been in Black America? Most searches are illegal, but in this case, they had me dead to rights. So on that day, at that time and that moment, for no search to happen?

God had a plan. It wasn't me. It was Him.

I was nineteen when my father died and I chose to take off on a dangerous trajectory. I ascended rapidly, to the point where I was flying at forty-four thousand feet. By the time I reached age twenty-one, the landing gear was coming out. I didn't want to keep flying. I couldn't.

. . .

Stress and paranoia can kill you slowly, like a disease. You never know where the threat might come from—a relative, an acquaintance, a close friend, an enemy. Duck, Meco, and my immediate crew were rock solid, but we did business with a much wider circle of individuals. I had known Cactus since kindergarten, and he might have killed me for the couple thousand I beat him for in a dice game. Now think about what a slept rock would do for a couple hundred thousand.

We took penitentiary chances every day, risking it all to try and gain a better position. I still have nightmares about it. Other nights I can't even get to sleep because I'm thinking about what might have happened. A few bad breaks and I could be serving life.

I look at pictures that we took in clubs when we were young and see guys I once talked to every day. Sometimes I feel survivor's guilt that I'm where I'm at and these men never made it out of Glenville. Some guys from those pictures are doing twenty years. I really loved them and I wish I could have all of them with me at Klutch, not just a few. The brotherhood that we built, the care and the bond, those things should last forever.

Looking at those pictures also reassures me that nothing was given to me. I embrace my journey, which makes all the criticism and backlash I get in my current position irrelevant. People always ask me, "Rich, aren't you mad about what so-and-so said about you?" Not at all, because I came through the fire. I came through things I can't even talk about, but those experiences allow me to stand tall among the trees, no matter what room I'm in.

Look, there's nothing I haven't done. Let your imagination run. But I'm telling you, that's not the be-all and end-all. A lot of times when you're in the streets, you're doing things for the "right now." Young people only see what's in front of them, and don't have an understanding of what's behind that wall. You can't even imagine what's behind that wall. That's why we have to believe that we are more than what we're told we are. We have to have faith in that idea, even when we can't see it yet. All I saw beyond my block was more blocks just like it, more Cleveland. But I couldn't accept a life of dead ends. I believed I was built for more. We all are.

. . .

In the spring of 2001, I had just bought a pair of Adidas from a store called Walton's, white low-tops with three red-suede stripes and a strap over the top of the ankle. In my mind, I put them together with a sky-blue Warren Moon Houston Oilers throwback, because Moon's number "1" had a red outline around it. I had a trip to Atlanta coming up, and the day of the flight I assembled that combination and headed for the airport.

My man D Hodge booked the tickets. For some reason, he scheduled the flight out of the Akron airport instead of Cleveland. OK, cool. I drove the Camry over there, went through security, and walked to my gate.

I was waiting to board the plane when a few tall young dudes walked up to me. The kid in the front wore a Mike Vick jersey, from the Falcons, but it was a replica with a big ironed-on "7" on the front.

"What kind of jersey is that?" the kid in the Vick asked me.

"This is an authentic Warren Moon jersey, from the Oilers. I got a whole bunch like these if you want, I'm available 24/7/365 for the most part. Here's my card, just ask for Rich, you won't have no problems. So what's your name?"

I stuck my hand out. He gave me a pound. "What up, Rich," he said. "I'm LeBron."

# EPILOGUE

In 2002, not long after I met LeBron, Candace gave birth to our daughter, Reonna. Our baby girl inspired some much-needed maturation in me, plus she brought another, unexpected gift:

My mother came back into my life.

Peaches wasn't about to ignore her baby boy's first child. She came to visit us at my house in South Euclid, and it was clear that she was trying to get herself together. All of her fantastic Peaches personality was flowing, without the addict's behavior. She was attentive, funny, caring, everything I remembered from the good times. I knew she probably wasn't totally clean, but I didn't care. I asked Mom to stay with us in South Euclid until we could find her a spot of her own.

I wasn't worried about her substance issues putting Reonna in danger. Mom never came around us when she was high. Also, I had spent so many years without her, I just wanted her around. I didn't care what else she was doing.

Mom went to drug counseling sessions, then worked as a counselor herself. I helped her buy a few properties where she rented out rooms for people who were trying to get back on their feet. In certain moments I was really proud of her, which was a new feeling for me.

We found Mom her own apartment, then a house, and she continued to flourish. I was happy just to see her enjoying life, living on her own, having her own car, not sleeping on somebody's couch or in their basement. I was happy for her to have stability. I saw a few signs that she had not totally kicked her drug habit, but I just told her, "Mom, please do whatever you do in the privacy of your own home. Don't be out on the street with it." Not only because I wanted her to be safe, but because that could make me more of a target. Somebody could have used her situation against me.

I did all I could to give Mom happiness, the same as my father did. I was at peace with who she was and her role in my life.

. . .

LeBron and I hit it off from the moment we met. He was headed to Atlanta to watch the NCAA tournament, and once we got down there, we hung out. When we returned home, he and his boys started coming over to my house to chill and play video games.

Our vibe was organic—our mothers went through the same struggles with addiction, and his part of Akron was another version of
Glenville. I knew his friend Maverick from playing Catholic school
basketball. I also think LeBron was intrigued with how I carried
myself. When a group of us went to a club, we walked right in. VIP
section? No problem. I knew about restaurants that most guys
never heard of. LeBron saw that I was independent and had my
own thing going. I wasn't asking for anything and I didn't have an
angle. We just enjoyed being around each other. Everything was
authentic and real. I understood the depth of who he was, the
good and the bad of it. That's the core of our relationship, and the
core of my work today with Black athletes. Our minds often move
in the same ways, on an individual and collective basis. I've been
through so many of the experiences that define the hard side of
Black life in America, I can always find common ground with
someone, no matter who they are. And, of course, I've worked
with athletes who are white, athletes from Europe and Asia and all
over the world, too. The Black American experience resonates
with so many people, so many lives. In an elevated way, the story
of our struggles is the basic essence of the human struggle. Every
person on this planet needs love, dignity, and purpose.

In the spring of 2003, a few months before he was drafted
Number One by the Cleveland Cavaliers, LeBron called my phone.
I went over to see him at a place he was living in with Randy Mims,
on Moreley Avenue in Akron. He was about to sign his first Nike
deal.

We made some small talk, and then he asked for my Social Security number.

"What are you talking about? I just got my credit cleaned up," I told him. I trusted LeBron and knew he wasn't into anything shady, but my hood reflex was to protect myself from falling into a trap.

"Don't worry," LeBron said. "I'll tell you later."

A few weeks went by. Peaches was staying at my house and one day she told me I had received a check in the mail. When we opened the envelope, the check was from King James Inc., for a couple thousand dollars. It had a pay stub attached. Mom showed me how to decipher the pay period. The salary added up to forty-eight thousand dollars per year.

I called LeBron immediately and asked what was going on. What was I supposed to be doing for this money?

"I don't know yet," he said. "But ever since I met you, you've just kept it real with me. I know I got to have you around me. Right now I don't have a role for you. We'll figure it out."

. . .

Mom always fought the demons of the time she couldn't get back. Later, as I had more children, I had to tell her, "Mom, why are you worrying about the past? What you're putting into the grandkids now, being present, that's the most important thing."

But I could tell she couldn't get fully over it. I didn't know how to respond to her pain, or even how to understand it, until I tried to put myself in the shoes of a mother who abandoned her children for a drug. Then I think I could feel it. I had more sympathy.

I needed to make a run to Philadelphia to pick up jerseys from the Mitchell & Ness store. I didn't have anybody to ride with me, so Mom decided to come along. As we were getting ready to pull out I said, "Hold on a minute, we gotta grab the strap."

Peaches was no stranger to pistols. My dad was a gunslinger. So she held the 9mm and rode with it in her purse all the way to Philly and back. It was a great trip—we hit 80 East in my Camry and listened to music, stopped for food, and just talked about life. It felt like recovering a piece of my childhood.

Even better was bringing her to the 2016 championship parade in Cleveland. By now I was an agent, and had helped arrange LeBron's return home from the Miami Heat. I was just coming off my client Ben Simmons being drafted Number One. I rode with my mom and my kids on a float. She never stopped talking about that experience.

A few months after the parade, I got a call from my sister Brandie. I had just bought my first house in Los Angeles and was working out at the gym.

"They found Mom unresponsive. She's at the hospital."

I grasped for the calm that had served me so well in the past. *Peaches is strong. She's been through worse. She'll pull through.*

I was carrying a box of stuff up the steps into my new house when Brandie rang my phone again, hysterical.

Mom was gone, at age sixty-one.

Oddly enough, I smiled before I started crying.

· · ·

I think about you often, Mom. Mostly when I'm around my own children. I walked into my son Richie's room one morning before I left on a trip, when he was still asleep. When I rested my hand on his back, I felt your presence—and your absence. It's a weird balance, because I feel power in the strength I was forced to develop by your absence. As I touched Richie, and I felt my love for him as an almost physical sensation running through my body, I knew you felt that same love for me. I feel your love more strongly now than when you were alive. The longer you're gone, the more I see you for who you truly were.

In some ways I appreciate everything that happened. What we went through helped remove all weakness from me. It gave me determination, calm, and confidence. Without you, I wouldn't be where I am today. I want the world to know that I love you completely, without any caveats or qualifications. I understand what you dealt with and why you did the things you did. The stereotype about mothers who use drugs is they don't love their children. But I felt your love during those times we were able to spend together, whether that was in a roach-infested apartment or at a championship parade. And I feel your love today in the knowledge that you kept me from seeing you at your lowest. I have no memories of you under the influence of drugs. I never witnessed your lips touch a crack pipe. You protected me from having to live with any of that.

My only regret is that before you left this world, I didn't get to tell you that I'm all right. This has nothing to do with my career, because being successful is different from being emotionally healthy. What I mean is that although your absence hurt me as a kid, you didn't damage me permanently. I do have scars, but they're not from you. My wounds were inflicted by the same forces that left you unable to be the mother you wanted to be. I want you to know that when all is said and done, you didn't injure your child. It's not my place to say that I forgive you—every son owes his life to his mother. But you don't have to be sorry about anything. I'm in a great place, Mom. I understand, and I love you.

. . .

There was a point in my NBA agenting career when people realized just how much my team and I intended to disrupt the system, when they tried to get rid of me. The NCAA passed a rule saying that you needed a college degree to represent players entering the draft. While it lasted, which wasn't long, people called it the Rich Paul Rule. Basically, a lot of people were upset that someone like me had the audacity to unapologetically represent some of the biggest stars in the sport. They were upset that I rejected their criteria for admission and worked to remake a system that historically has only benefitted them. And they're threatened by the fact that they can never have what I have, which are my experiences. So they tried to outlaw me. That's what the temporary Rich Paul Rule was about.

What they thought were disqualifications became my selling points. College or not, I know I'm as well prepared as anybody for the business I'm in. After everything I've endured, there's very little their system can teach me. Nobody else in my business knows what it's like to put two and two together out of zero. I know what it's like to serve somebody, and watch out for the police, and watch out for the rival crews, and watch out for the jackers, *and* watch out for the people I'm serving because they might have a pistol. I know how to keep working even if in a split second, my life might be over.

Not a day goes by that I don't remember that life. How could I forget? I gained a lot of advantages from those experiences, for sure, but it shouldn't have had to be that way—because it came at such a high cost. I don't want anybody else to experience what me and my guys went through. I'm still traumatized by it, in ways that are hard for me to even admit to myself. The visual memory of things we saw, not even things we actually did—those scenes stay with us for life. We never added up all that trauma in the moment, we were too busy trying to keep it moving. All these years later, those of us who experienced those things are no different than soldiers who survived a war but can never forget it.

There is no safer neighborhood in America than where I live

now, in Beverly Hills. But I don't know where I'm more comfortable, here or back on St. Clair. In Beverly Hills, I don't hear dogs barking, sirens, people yelling or arguing. That feels weird, because chaos and danger still feel like home to me. Peace puts me on edge.

. . .

One of my all-time favorite Jay-Z songs is a deep cut called "Lucky Me." Jay is talking about how success brings envy, jealousy, and danger, and about how people think his life is perfect, but he's dealing with more than they could ever know. It's a powerful, mournful, and somewhat sarcastic song, with a hook that goes: *You only know what you see / You don't understand what it takes to be me.*

That's exactly how I feel about my life. There's a narrative out there that LeBron gave me everything based on a Warren Moon jersey, but very few people know or respect what I had to go through to reach that point, or what I've done since then to reach where I am now. This disrespect comes from preconceived notions about Black men who come from the bottom. All my clients know I sold dope. Society can accept that poor Black environments instill a hunger, drive, and savvy that produces great athletes. It's long overdue for society to accept that we can produce just as many great executives, too.

I don't want my legacy to be money, or fame, or my representation of sports superstars. I hope my legacy is that my type of journey becomes the norm.

Yes, my story is one in a million. But what if I'd had the exact same talent, the same brain, but came from a wealthy white family? My success would have almost been guaranteed. Yet for a kid from St. Clair to do something big, I had to have what amounts to a cosmic accident. That's what we need to change. There are still too many young Black people with ambition and genius, but no platform. Imagine having a mind that's free, and yet your existence is trapped.

To all my people currently risking your lives and your freedom under the circumstances of the ghetto, I'm here to tell you that you didn't get a fair chance. I feel so deeply for y'all. I understand why you might make wrong choices, facing the mountains you have to climb just because of the color of your skin or the place you were born. But don't get me wrong. You might be thinking, *Rich made it out hustling, so can I.* I'm telling you, it's not worth the risk. If things go left, you probably won't get a second chance. Think about how lucky I had to be. And how lucky am I, really? I lost my mom, my dad, my childhood. I lost my sense of perspective about right and wrong, about what's truly valuable in life. I lost my innocence. You can't rely on luck to make it. Rely on yourself, your effort, your talent, and the knowledge that the journey itself provides what you need to succeed.

My journey began on the East Side of Cleveland, Ohio, at the corner of 125th and Edmonton, in a store owned by a man's man who taught me how to create my own luck.

## ACKNOWLEDGMENTS

Family is everything to me. By now everyone knows how much I love and appreciate my mother and father. I also want to thank my sister Brandie Bohlen; my brother, Meco Bohlen; my sister Nicole Paul; my grandmothers Ruth Martin and Johnnie Mae Paul; Ozelle Thompson a.k.a. Uncle Joe; Aunt Linda and Uncle Warren Franklin; and my uncles Lance and Kevin Martin.

There are so many people from the Glenville community to remember and name, but just know I love and appreciate all of you, and I represent every step of the way. All of you helped me survive, holding my hand as a kid and then holding me accountable as an adult.

Thank you to everyone who shared their memories for this book: Brandie, Meco, Candace, Uncle Lance, Nicole, Eric Bledsoe,

Maverick Carter, Fara Leff, Aaron Nichols, Edward Givens, Mike Ivey, Damon Glymph, Martin McCoy, Mike Woods, Mrs. Pymn, Mr. Francioli, Mr. DiGeronimo, Wink, and Willie Wild.

I've been part of some great teams in my life, and the squad for this book was amazing, starting with my literary agent, Byrd Leavell, and my not-so-secret weapon Adam Mendelsohn. Georgia Breit, who leads my office, kept the trains running on time. My editor, Chris Jackson, elevated my thoughts and inspired new insights. My co-writer, Jesse Washington, took me places I did not expect to go.

Finally, I'd like to thank my children: Reonna, Richie, and Zane. I hope you always feel the presence of Peaches and Big Rich through my love for you.

ABOUT THE AUTHOR

RICH PAUL is the founder and CEO of Klutch Sports Group, the powerhouse sports agency representing some of the biggest athletes in professional sports. In 2019, he was named *GQ*'s "Power Broker of the Year" and "The King Maker" on the cover of *Sports Illustrated*. *Variety* named Paul to their "Variety500" list of the most influential business leaders shaping the global media industry, and *Time* recognized Klutch on its first-ever list of TIME100 Most Influential Companies. Paul has been a partner in the LRMR Marketing Agency since 2003, and launched the performance sportswear brand Klutch Athletics in 2023. He is the father of Reonna, Richie, and Zane and lives in Los Angeles and Cleveland.

## ABOUT THE TYPE

This book was set in Dante, a typeface designed by Giovanni Mardersteig (1892–1977). Conceived as a private type for the Officina Bodoni in Verona, Italy, Dante was originally cut only for hand composition by Charles Malin, the famous Parisian punch cutter, between 1946 and 1952. Its first use was in an edition of Boccaccio's *Trattatello in laude di Dante* that appeared in 1954. The Monotype Corporation's version of Dante followed in 1957. Though modeled on the Aldine type used for Pietro Cardinal Bembo's treatise *De Aetna* in 1495, Dante is a thoroughly modern interpretation of that venerable face.